MW01221679

Poeti–c Art

The poetic cart
has two wheels
equal
and efficient

what to say
and how

neither
is superior
to the other

if either one
is missing
there is
no cart
moving

—ARUDRA (BHAGAVATULA SANKARA SASTRI)

Music, Pictures, and Stories
A Poetry Anthology

HOLT, RINEHART AND WINSTON

A Harcourt Education Company

Austin • Orlando • Chicago • New York • Toronto • London • San Diego

Staff Credits

EDITORIAL

Executive Editor

Katie Vignery

Editor

Carolyn Logan

Copyediting: Mary Malone, *Copyediting Supervisor;* Elizabeth Dickson, *Senior Coypeditor;* Emily Force, Jennifer Kirkland, *Copyeditors*

Project Administration: Marie Price, *Managing Editor;* Lori De La Garza, *Editorial Finance Manager;* Michael Neibergall, *Administrative Managing Editor;* Janet Riley, *Senior Editorial Coordinator;* Brian Kachmar, *Assistant Editorial Coordinator;* Benny Carmona III, *Editorial Ops Coordinator;* Margaret Sanchez, *Word Processing Supervisor;* Casey Kelley, Joie Pickett, *Word Processors*

Editorial Permissions: Carrie Jones, *Supervisor of Contracts, Copyrights, Permissions*

DESIGN

Image Acquisitions: Curtis Riker, *Director;* Jeannie Taylor, *Photo Research Supervisor;* Rick Benavides, *Photo Researcher*

Graphic Services: Kristen Darby, *Director;* Jeff Robinson, *Senior Ancillary Designer*

Cover Design: Richard Metzger, *Design Director;* Sunday Patterson, *Designer*

PRODUCTION

Beth Prevelige, *Prepress Manager*

Carol Trammel, *Production Supervisor*

Michael Roche, *Senior Production Coordinator*

MANUFACTURING/INVENTORY

Shirley Cantrell, *Manufacturing Supervisor*

Deborah Hilst, *Inventory Supervisor*

Copyright © by Holt, Rinehart and Winston

All rights reserved. No part of this publication may be reproduced or transmitted in any form or by any means, electronic or mechanical, including photocopy, recording, or any information storage and retrieval system, without permission in writing from the publisher.

Requests for permission to make copies of any part of the work should be mailed to the following address: Permissions Department, Holt, Rinehart and Winston, 10801 N. MoPac Expressway, Building 3, Austin, Texas 78759.

Acknowledgments and other credits appear on pages 187–188, which are an extension of the copyright page.

HRW is a trademark of Holt, Rinehart and Winston, registered in the United States of America and/or other jurisdictions.

Printed in the United States of America

ISBN 0-03-067541-3

2 3 4 5 6 043 04 03

Table of Contents

The Elements of Poetry

Why do poets write poetry?

Some poets say it is because they love words—the sound and feel of words on the tongue, the rhythms words create when they are arranged in this way or that. Other poets speak of the pictures words offer for your imagination. Some poets have a message they want you to hear and act upon; some write for those who need someone to champion their cause. Poets may want to make the world a better, safer, happier place. Other poets want to tell a story. Many poets simply want to tell you about themselves—about their sadness, their hope, their delight and happiness. Some poets really cannot say why they write poetry; it is just something that they *must* do.

Why should we bother to read or write poetry?

Poetry has the power to alter the way you see the world. A poem may show you the freshness of air after the rain and inspire you to think of the natural world in a different way. Poetry can have a powerful effect on your emotions, changing a dark mood and coaxing the sun from behind the clouds. A poem can inspire you to drive the soccer ball into the goal, to test yourself in other ways. Poetry sharpens our awareness of life and deepens our response to it. We can never grasp the full glory, terror, strangeness, or sadness of our world, but poems catch shards, glints, and glimpses of it.

When you write a poem, you can express your thoughts and feelings. That way, many years from now, when you have grown into your adult self, you will remember the way you felt in this moment.

There is really no set way to learn to write poetry—no school for poetry. Poets can devote lifetimes to their art, teaching themselves by reading, writing, experimenting, and arguing with other poets. Nevertheless, poetry, like any art, involves basic techniques and principles. Some of these you already know because they are part of your experience with language. For example, you already know about words that rhyme:

> Hickory, dickory, dock!
> The mouse ran up the clock;

For years you've been playing with words that start with the same, tongue-tickling sound, as in Simple Simon or Peter Piper and his peck of pickled peppers.

When you learn to play the guitar, you learn chords and rhythms. Similarly, when you read and write poetry, you learn figurative language, expressive strategies, and rhythms.

This book will introduce you to the ways in which the poetic elements have been used by contemporary poets. You will be able to appreciate their experiments and try some of their techniques yourself.

Sometimes poetry frightens people because they "can't understand it." "What does it *mean*?" they worry. The truth is, a poem will mean something different for each reader because each reader brings different feelings and experiences to the reading of a poem.

Many people think poetry is a lonesome art for the most solitary, sullen, and lovesick among us. Certainly most poets need some quiet time to compose and read, but poetry has never liked being left out of life. It wants to be invited to the party, to the soccer field, to your neighborhood, street, and home.

When you read *Music, Pictures, and Stories*, you are opening a door and inviting poetry into your life. You will not be sorry.

The Music of Poetry

You may prefer to listen to the latest songs on a CD rather than read a book of poetry. However, if you read the lyrics of a song, you will realize that many musicians are gifted poets. The origins of poetry are deeply entwined with music. Ancient Greek poets recited their poems while a musician accompanied them on a lyre, a small, harplike, stringed instrument. What we call "lyric poetry"—songlike poems that express feeling—can be traced to these ancient Greek performances. Today, the lyrics of ballads find their way into poetry anthologies, and some popular musicians have found song lyrics in poetry books.

Poets know that words alone can create musical effects and have several strategies they can use to play with the sound of words. One of these sound effects is **rhythm,** which is a repeated sound pattern. Some poems have a regular pattern of sound, and we say that this is the poem's **meter**. Other poems have a rhythm that is close to the rhythms of ordinary speech. This kind of poetic rhythm is called **free verse**.

There are other sound effects that a poet can use. **Onomatopoeia** (än′ō•mat′ō•pē′ə) is a long word with a simple meaning: words that imitate the sound something makes. For example, *whippoorwill* is an onomatopoeic word because it imitates the sound that a bird makes. *Boom, sizzle,* and *whish* are other examples. When poets, or writers or speakers, repeat the *s*ame *s*ound or letter in *s*everal word*s*, they are using **alliteration,** as you can hear in the repeated *s* sound. Another familiar sound effect is a **refrain,** which is a repeated word or phrase. You may be more familiar with refrains in songs, but this sound effect is a favorite of poets as well.

As you explore the poetry in this chapter, read each poem aloud and listen for the music of the poetry.

SHEL SILVERSTEIN (1930–1999)

Hector the Collector

Hector the Collector
Collected bits of string,
Collected dolls with broken heads
And rusty bells that would not ring.
5   Pieces out of picture puzzles,
Bent-up nails and ice-cream sticks,
Twists of wires, worn-out tires,
Paper bags and broken bricks.
Old chipped vases, half shoelaces,
10   Gatlin' guns° that wouldn't shoot,
Leaky boats that wouldn't float
And stopped-up horns that wouldn't toot.
Butter knives that had no handles,
Copper keys that fit no locks,
15   Rings that were too small for fingers,
Dried-up leaves and patched-up socks.
Worn-out belts that had no buckles.
'Lectric trains that had no tracks.
Airplane models, broken bottles,
20   Three-legged chairs and cups with cracks.
Hector the Collector
Loved these things with all his soul—
Loved them more than shining diamonds,
Loved them more than glistenin' gold.
25   Hector called to all the people,
"Come and share my treasure trunk!"
And all the silly sightless people
Came and looked . . . and called it junk.

10. Gatlin' guns: Gatling guns, a type of early machine gun.

MEET THE *Poet*

SHEL SILVERSTEIN

"I never planned to write or draw for kids," Shel Silverstein confided to an interviewer. Silverstein joked that the girls paid no attention to him, so in order to have something to do, he began to draw and write. Silverstein was a successful cartoonist, drawing cartoons for magazines, when a friend "practically dragged me, kicking and screaming" into the role of a writer and illustrator of children's books. It turned out that Silverstein had a gift for writing poems silly and serious and sometimes a little strange, which both children and adults would love and remember. *Where the Sidewalk Ends* and his later collections *A Light in the Attic* and *Falling Up* were very successful. These

collections have led readers to compare Silverstein to Dr. Seuss, who also combined poetry and drawings, and Edward Lear, whose poems still enchant readers.

It may strike you that "Hector the Collector" ends on a sad note. Silverstein often avoided happy endings in his poems so that young readers would not finish a poem thinking, "Why can't I be this happy all the time, too?" However, Silverstein's poems did not all end on a sad note—he created all sorts of endings, from the happy to the sad.

PHILIP BOOTH (1925–   )

Crossing

STOP   LOOK   LISTEN
as gate stripes swing down,
count the cars hauling distance
upgrade° through town:

5   warning whistle, bellclang,
engine eating steam,
engineer waving,
a fast-freight dream:
B&M boxcar,

10   boxcar again,
Frisco gondola,°
eight-nine-ten,
Erie and Wabash,
Seaboard, U.P.,

15   Pennsy tankcar,
twenty-two, three,
Phoebe Snow, B&O,
thirty-four, five,
Santa Fe cattle

20   shipped alive,
red cars, yellow cars,
orange cars, black,
Youngstown steel
down to Mobile

25   on Rock Island track,
fifty-nine, sixty,

4. **upgrade:** uphill.
11. **gondola** (gän'dō•lə): freight car with low sides and no top.

hoppers° of coke,°

Anaconda copper,

hotbox° smoke,

30   *eighty-eight,*

red-ball freight,

Rio Grande,

Nickel Plate,

Hiawatha,

35   Lackawanna,

rolling fast

and loose,

ninety-seven,

coal car,

40   boxcar,

CABOOSE!

27. hoppers: freight cars whose bottoms open to unload cargo.
    coke: processed coal which burns with a high heat.
29. hotbox: overheated bearing or axle.

MEET THE *Poet*

PHILIP BOOTH

Philip Booth lives in the same house he lived in as a child. In fact, the Maine house has been in Booth's family for five generations. A feeling for and a sense of place—of the surrounding environment—is important for Booth and for his poetry.

One way to learn to write poetry is to study with an established, successful poet. That is what Philip Booth did when he studied poetry with Robert Frost, an important U.S. poet. Like Frost, Booth is known for his use of New England settings—sea, woods, and fields—in his poetry. Like Frost, Booth became a teacher of poetry himself.

Keeping notes is a way many poets gather the material they need for their poems. Booth has been keeping notebooks for over fifty years. He considers the notes an important part of his writing process. In one such note, Booth tells himself to "make *music.*"

Another entry from one of Booth's notebooks best sums up his life as a poet: "Writing poems is not a career but a lifetime of looking into, and listening to, how words see."

DONALD HALL (1928–   )

Valentine

Chipmunks jump, and
Greensnakes slither.
Rather burst than
Not be with her.

5   Bluebirds fight, but
Bears are stronger.
We've got fifty
Years or longer.

Hoptoads hop, but
10 Hogs are fatter.
Nothing else but
Us can matter.

Ox Cart Man

In October of the year,
he counts potatoes dug from the brown field,
counting the seed, counting
the cellar's portion out,
5   and bags the rest on the cart's floor.

He packs wool sheared in April, honey
in combs, linen, leather
tanned from deerhide
and vinegar in a barrel
10 hooped by hand at the forge's fire.

He walks by his ox's head, ten days
to Portsmouth Market, and sells potatoes,
and the bag that carried potatoes,
flaxseed, birch brooms, maple sugar, goose
15 feathers, yarn.

When the cart is empty he sells the cart.
When the cart is sold he sells the ox,
harness and yoke, and walks
homes, his pockets heavy
20 with the year's coin for salt and taxes,

and at home by fire's light in November cold
stitches new harness
for next year's ox in the barn,
and carves the yoke, and saws planks
25 building the cart again.

MEET THE *Poet*

DONALD HALL

Donald Hall grew up in a home that was filled with the sound of poetry. His mother read poetry aloud. His grandfather recited poetry all day while doing his farm chores, never repeating a poem. Others in the family wrote poetry. Therefore it is no surprise that Hall began writing poetry when he was twelve years old. He has

been so successful that a list of his poetry and children's stories fills several pages. Hall has carried on the family tradition and has read his poetry in more than a thousand places—from colleges and schools to prisons.

After many years as a teacher, Hall decided to buy the land his grandfather had farmed, live there, and write poetry full-time. He keeps a strict writing schedule, getting up before dawn to work. He may craft a poem for years, working on it now and then until he is satisfied. Hall believes that poems spring from all the experiences of a writer's life. Sometimes when young people write poems, they want to keep the poem to themselves. However, a completed poem, Hall says, is not private, secret writing. Once completed, poems should be shared because poems can connect people to one another.

JANE O. WAYNE (1938–   )

In Praise of Zigzags

For a Girl Failing Geometry

Maybe she does her homework
the way she does her chores.
She moves quickly when she vacuums,
forgetting corners in the living room,
5   repeating others,
zigzags recklessly across the carpet,
raising those pale tracks
behind her in the wool, crossing
and recrossing them. And not once
10   does geometry cross her mind.
Outside she wanders aimlessly
behind the lawnmower,
rolls toward the middle of the lawn,
then doubles back.
15   For a while, she'll follow straight lines—
the fence, the hedge, the walk—
then go off on a tangent, spiraling
around the birch or the maple.
When she finishes,
20   she leaves the lawnmower out, leaves
a trail of unmown strips and crisscrosses,
her scribbling on the lawn
like a line of thought that's hard to follow.
As far as she's concerned
25   the shortest distance between two points
is confining.

The Eavesdropper

That small girl crouched
on the top steps to listen
is still waiting to hear her name
on their lips, to come alive
5   like a deck of cards
shuffled in their downstairs hands.

She's still motionless
outside the living room, straining
to catch some hint
10   that no one drops, still in that hallway
dwelling on their talk
as a thumb does a rough fingernail.

MEET THE *Poet*

JANE O. WAYNE

Jane O. Wayne began writing in grade school by recording her thoughts and secrets in private diaries. Writing was a way to deal with those times when she felt like an outsider. Then, in her late teens, Wayne began writing poetry. Since then she has had many of her poems published in books and magazines. When she is not writing and teaching others to write, Wayne travels. She has spent months in exotic places—Turkey, Peru, and Ecuador. She even spent a year sailing around the world by freighter.

For Wayne, writing a poem is like stepping into a photograph and exploring its sounds, smells, and sights, and the emotions it brings out. Wayne also compares poems to jokes. She believes that at the first reading, a poem should surprise its reader with its ideas and the music of its words—just as a joke catches a listener by surprise. Although a joke may not be as funny the second time you hear it, a good poem gets better each time you read it.

Wayne encourages students to read poetry aloud and listen for its music—the sound and rhythm of the words and phrases. These express the emotions people feel but often do not talk about—love, loss, loneliness, or joy—and do not necessarily have to be understood to be enjoyed and appreciated.

ROBERT BLY (1926–   )

Things My Brother and I Could Do

For W. S.

Well there's no end of things to do.

We could go out and catch gophers.
We could read books.
We could pick the mud off tractor tires.

5   We could think about a pheasant falling.
We could think about Father falling.
We could see where he fell.

It was late one night, and he fell down
And hit his head on a boot scraper—
10 He didn't die—saying good-bye to others.

We could wonder about the War.
We could think about Bertha, who did die.
We could think about her daughter, who lived with us.

We could think about why her face was so thin.

Seeing the Eclipse in Maine

It started about noon. On top of Mount Batte,
We were all exclaiming. Someone had a cardboard
And a pin, and we all cried out when the sun
Appeared in tiny form on the notebook cover.

5   It was hard to believe. The high school teacher
We'd met called it a pinhole camera,
People in the Renaissance loved to do that.
And when the moon had passed partly through

We saw on a rock underneath a fir tree,
10   Dozens of crescents—made the same way—
Thousands! Even our straw hats produced
A few as we moved them over the bare granite.

We shared chocolate, and one man from Maine
Told a joke. Suns were everywhere—at our feet.

MEET THE *Poet*

ROBERT BLY

Robert Bly, and the rest of his class, fell in love with a high school teacher who recited poetry. Although convinced that poetry was a good thing, Bly kept his love for poetry secret until he again fell in love, this time with a woman who wrote poetry. He wrote a poem to impress her—it didn't— but he surprised himself with that poem. He realized that in putting the words on paper, he had said more than he had intended to say. Because of this experience, Bly believes that each person has inside him or her a voice that is observant, wise, and witty—a poetic voice. To let that voice have its say is to begin to write poetry. He tries to write every day, giving his poetic voice time to make itself heard.

Bly wants to write poetry that helps connect people to their world and their emotions. He is interested in how people think and feel about nature. He avoids difficult, formal language and appeals to readers' emotions. Bly believes that poetry can heal the pain in people's lives and lead them to make better decisions. He carried out this belief when he joined with other poets to write about the Vietnam War in the 1960s.

VICTOR HERNÁNDEZ CRUZ
(1949–   )

The Latest Latin Dance Craze

FIRST
You throw your head back twice
Jump out onto the floor like a
Kangaroo
5   Circle the floor once
Doing fast scissor work with your
Legs
Next
Dash towards the door
10 Walking in a double cha cha cha
Open the door and glide down
The stairs like a swan
Hit the street
Run at least ten blocks
15 Come back in through the same
Door
Doing a mambo-minuet
Being careful that you don't fall
And break your head on that one
20 You have just completed your first
Step.

Problems with Hurricanes

A campesino looked at the air
And told me:
With hurricanes it's not the wind
or the noise or the water.
5   I'll tell you he said:
it's the mangoes, avocados
Green plantains and bananas
flying into town like projectiles.

How would your family
10   feel if they had to tell
The generations that you
got killed by a flying
Banana.

Death by drowning has honor
15   If the wind picked you up
and slammed you
Against a mountain boulder
This would not carry shame
But
20   to suffer a mango smashing
Your skull
or a plantain hitting your
Temple at 70 miles per hour
is the ultimate disgrace.

25   The campesino takes off his hat—
As a sign of respect
towards the fury of the wind

And says:
Don't worry about the noise

30   Don't worry about the water
Don't worry about the wind—
If you are going out
beware of mangoes
And all such beautiful

35   sweet things.

MEET THE *Poet*

VICTOR HERNÁNDEZ CRUZ

"My family life was full of music, guitars and conga drums, maracas and songs. My mother sang songs. Even when it was five below zero in New York she sang warm tropical ballads."

Perhaps as a result of this musical family life, Victor Hernández Cruz writes poetry that is full of a particularly personal music. Cruz was born in Puerto Rico and immigrated to New York City when he was five years old. Cruz's lively poetry records a life lived in two languages. His poetry also tells of life in two contrasting worlds: a tropical island and a metal-and-concrete city.

As a child, Cruz listened to his grandfather's stories and to novels read chapter by chapter, absorbing the music of the spoken language of Puerto Rico. In New York City, he grew aware of the music of a large city—street sounds, a mixture of languages, English spoken with many accents and in many dialects. Cruz takes the details his five senses record and blends these together to create poetry that sings with rhythm and repetition and that abounds in his personal, energetic music.

THEODORE ROETHKE (1908–1963)

Highway: Michigan

Here from the field's edge we survey
The progress of the jaded.° Mile
On mile of traffic from the town
Rides by, for at the end of day
5   The time of workers is their own.

They jockey for position on
The strip reserved for passing only.
The drivers from production lines
Hold to advantage dearly won.
10   They toy with death and traffic fines.

Acceleration is their need:
A mania keeps them on the move
Until the toughest nerves are frayed.
They are the prisoners of speed
15   Who flee in what their hands have made.

The pavement smokes when two cars meet
And steel rips through conflicting steel.
We shiver at the siren's blast.
One driver, pinned beneath the seat,
20   Escapes from the machine at last.

2. **jaded** (jād'id): weary, tired; worn out.

THEODORE ROETHKE

When he was young, Theodore Roethke worked hard to be accepted by those who thought that "brains were sissies." He became tough and strong, like the gangsters that fascinated him. At the same time, he was desperate for a friend who would listen to his dreams for the future.

As he grew older, Roethke's friend was his poetry, and poetry and the teaching of poetry became his career. Roethke learned to write through imitation. He once wrote that "imitation, conscious imitation, is one of the great methods, perhaps THE method of learning to write. . . ." He came out at the end of this period a poet who could stop imitating and create his unique poetry.

Roethke decided early on that his main subject matter would be himself. Roethke kept notes—his pockets were crammed with bits of paper. He filled over two hundred notebooks with conversations, childhood memories, criticism of himself and others, his thoughts, and poetry.

Roethke was an immensely popular and creative professor, and the advice he gave his students is still good today. "You've got to have rhythm," Roethke said; and "Don't be so guarded—let your mind buzz around."

MARTIN ESPADA (1957–   )

Courthouse Graffiti for Two Voices

Jimmy C.
Greatest Car Thief Alive
Chelsea '88

Then what
5   are you doing
here?

Who Burns for the Perfection of Paper

At sixteen, I worked after high school hours
at a printing plant
that manufactured legal pads:
Yellow paper
5   stacked seven feet high
and leaning
as I slipped cardboard
between the pages,
then brushed red glue
10   up and down the stack.
No gloves: fingertips required
for the perfection of paper,
smoothing the exact rectangle.
Sluggish by 9 PM, the hands
15   would slide along suddenly sharp paper,
and gather slits thinner than the crevices
of the skin, hidden.
Then the glue would sting,
hands oozing
20   till both palms burned
at the punchclock.
Ten years later, in law school,
I knew that every legal pad
was glued with the sting of hidden cuts,
25   that every open lawbook
was a pair of hands
upturned and burning.

MEET THE *Poet*

MARTIN ESPADA

Martin Espada's father is a photographer, and Espada imitates a photographer as he writes his poems. Just as Espada's father

focused his camera lens to achieve a clear, sharp image, so Espada focuses on simile and metaphor, carefully selecting and putting words together to create his poetic image. Perhaps in appreciation of this process, photographs by Espada's father appear with the poems in *The Immigrant Iceboy's Bolero,* Espada's first published book of poetry.

Espada believes that all people should have a voice, particularly those whose stories are seldom heard—those who are powerless and struggle against injustice and misfortune. Espada brings his ability as an attorney and a teacher, as well as his gifts as a poet to this task. In "Who Burns for the Perfection of Paper," Espada recounts the painful work involved in binding legal pads. His poem reminds readers that every finished product they use contains someone's time and labor, and has perhaps inflicted small injuries. "Courthouse Graffiti for Two Voices" is a clear and precise snapshot of failure.

Espada wants his poetry to make his reader feel the pain of the voiceless people about whom he writes. He wants his words to name and condemn their hopeless conditions and through this, bring about change.

HAL SIROWITZ (1949–   )

Emergency Situation

I threw out your blue underwear,
Mother said. It had a hole in it.
No son of mine will ever be caught wearing that.
It's a reflection on me. It makes me look bad.

5   I know no one can see it. But you can't be sure.
Let's say you break your leg. You're rushed
to the hospital. The nurse takes off
your pants. She'll see it. The doctor
may not even put on a cast, because

10   he'll think you come from a poor family.
I didn't bring you up to embarrass me.
When you were little I dressed you up
as a girl. You were gorgeous.
You had curls hanging over your face.

15   But let's be honest. You're no longer cute.
You're too old to get away with anything.

MEET THE *Poet*

HAL SIROWITZ

In New York City, Hal Sirowitz is a poet with many fans. Performance artist, poet, and teacher, Sirowitz wanted to be a writer from an early age, and his salesman father supported his son's desire. However, not until he was thirty years old did Sirowitz settle on his subject matter—his mother. Sirowitz's mother was a strong-minded woman who loved her children and was determined to teach them the right way to do everything. She was Sirowitz's inspiration for his popular collection of poems called *Mother Said*. Although Sirowitz's mother is no longer alive, she continues to inspire her son's poetry, ensuring that Sirowitz does not have writer's block.

Sirowitz acquired his many fans when he began to perform his poems at poetry slams and readings. His performances were so popular that he went on to appear on television for global audiences. The poems from *Mother Said* have been translated into several languages and have met with warm responses from listeners who claim that their mothers told them the same things. Sometimes these fans suggest stories for his poetry, but Sirowitz stays true to the inner voice of his mother.

VINCE GOTERA (1952–   )

Beetle on a String

When I was a kid, I walked bugs on a leash.
This was in the Philippines, where my parents
and I moved when I was a toddler, trading
foggy San Francisco for Manila's typhoons.

5   Actually, it was an idyllic place for a child—
warm evenings drenched in the sweet scent
of sampaguita flowers, but most of all,
a huge universe of enthralling insects

filling the night with buzzing and clicks, strobe
10   flashes of their glow-in-the-dark wingflicks.
It was my father who showed me how to catch
a scarab beetle in the cup of your hand, wait

for the wings to subside and close, then loop a thread
between thorax and carapace, tying it off—
15   not too tight—to allow the insect to fly
on a two-foot-long lasso. I remember

how I would smile and laugh, maybe five
or six years old, as a beetle would circle my head
like a whirring kite, iridescent green in the sun,
20   the thread stretched almost to the breaking point.

At night, I would tie my beetles to the round knobs
on my dresser drawers and be soothed to sleep
by a lullaby of buzzing. By morning, the beetles
were always dead, weights hung on a string.

25   Those long nights must have been horrible.
    Straining your body to shift an immovable weight,
    unable to evade the swooping flight
    of predators, banging again and again hard

    against the dead wood, brought up short
30   by that unforgiving tether, cutting off
    your pulsing blood every time, the long tube
    of your heart quivering. It makes me shiver now

    to wonder what thoughtless boy holds my string?

MEET THE *Poet*

VINCE GOTERA

A poet who plays blues, rock, and jazz on his electric bass guitar—that is Vince Gotera. A poet who has lived in two vastly different

countries—the United States and the Philippines—that is also Gotera. Born in San Francisco, Gotera spent several years of his childhood in the Philippines. These are the childhood years that Gotera writes about in his poem "Beetle on a String."

After his college years, Gotera traded the lush tropical climate of the Philippines, abuzz with insects and scented with flowers, for the cold and often snow-covered plains of Iowa. There he is a professor of creative writing.

Like many writers of his generation, Gotera has written about the difficult Vietnam years; he also tells the stories of Filipino immigrants struggling to build lives in the United States.

Gotera not only writes poetry, but also edits two poetry journals, including the important journal *North American Review,* established in 1815.

If you look at a map, you will see that the Philippines is very far from San Francisco and even farther from Iowa. Yet Gotera, in his poetry and his teaching, has been able to build a bridge of words across that vast distance.

NAOMI SHIHAB NYE

If you ever talk with Naomi Shihab Nye, watch out. You may find yourself, or some of your words, in one of her poems. Many of Nye's poems clearly began as conversations. In fact, the idea of conversation is central to Nye's definition of poetry.

> Poetry is a conversation with the world; poetry is a conversation with the words on the page in which you allow those words to speak back to you; and poetry is a conversation with yourself.

To see what Nye means by this, look at "The Lost Parrot." This poem is like the script for a play. Many of the lines record a

conversation between the speaker, who is a teacher, and Carlos, one of her students. The teacher wants each student to write a poem about a dream, but all Carlos can contribute is the briefest of stories about his parrot, which has flown away. Oddly, Carlos responds the same way to all writing assignments. His subject is always the same: the parrot.

Notice how Nye's careful placement of the words emphasizes their dignity. Each comment has its own line, and each exchange is surrounded and framed by white space. Some of Carlos's comments are set off by themselves as if they are particularly important, perhaps more important than those of the the teacher. There are no quotation marks around the teacher's dialogue with Carlos; there is no "he said" or "I said" to help us keep track of who is speaking. As a result, we have to pay close attention to the exchange, and we have to pay even closer attention to Carlos's *words*. When words are carefully placed in a poem, their spacing tells us that they are urgent, are necessary to our understanding.

At the end of the poem, the voice of the poet-teacher takes over as she imagines a wild story in which Carlos finds and rescues the parrot. She seems to be so frustrated with Carlos's two-word poems that she is writing poems about the parrot herself. In discussing this poem, however, Nye has speculated that ". . . perhaps [Carlos] was right. For each of us, as the end suggests, the one real subject may be loss—what we love, and what we do when it leaves us." Carlos inspired in Nye a conversation with herself, and this poetic response shows us that Carlos's words are themselves poems.

As well as listening to what other people have to say or entering into conversation with them, Nye talks to herself—sometimes out loud. Nye thinks that we should all talk to ourselves and *listen* to ourselves more often. When Nye sits down to write, she enters into a conversation with the piece of paper, which is perhaps another way to converse with herself.

In her use of conversation—with the people around her, with herself, and with her environment—Nye builds on the experience of many previous poets who felt that poetry comes alive when poets pay attention to everything around them. However, Nye seems to have added a great capacity to listen. Through the sharing of her poems with others, she shows how a generous receptiveness to the world around her enlarges the conversation, for herself and for her readers.

NAOMI SHIHAB NYE (1952–   )

My Father and the Figtree

For other fruits my father was indifferent.
He'd point at the cherry trees and say,
"See those? I wish they were figs."
In the evenings he sat by my bed

5 weaving folktales like vivid little scarves.
They always involved a figtree.
Even when it didn't fit, he'd stick it in.
Once Joha was walking down the road and he saw a figtree.
Or, he tied his camel to a figtree and went to sleep.

10 Or, later when they caught and arrested him,
his pockets were full of figs.

At age six I ate a dried fig and shrugged.
"That's not what I'm talking about!" he said,
"I'm talking about a fig straight from the earth—

15 gift of Allah!—on a branch so heavy it touches the ground.
I'm talking about picking the largest fattest sweetest fig
in the world and putting it in my mouth."
(Here he'd stop and close his eyes.)

Years passed, we lived in many houses, none had fig trees.

20 We had lima beans, zucchini, parsley, beets.
"Plant one!" my mother said, but my father never did.
He tended garden half-heartedly, forgot to water,
let the okra get too big.
"What a dreamer he is. Look how many things he starts

25 and doesn't finish."

The last time he moved, I got a phone call.
My father, in Arabic, chanting a song I'd never heard.

"What's that?" I said.
"Wait till you see!"

30 He took me out back to the new yard.
There, in the middle of Dallas, Texas,
a tree with the largest, fattest, sweetest figs in the world.
"It's a figtree song!" he said,
plucking his fruits like ripe tokens,

35 emblems, assurance
of a world that was always his own.

Linked

My American grandmother said, I don't know,
oh I don't know, and my grandfather said, You'd better.
She took a little bow backwards: whatever you say.
Luckily I had two others across the sea who were mysteries.

5 My mother wrote her own early story down
in a red book which I found.
Saw movie. New dress.
When I was ten, I wanted her to complete the sentence.

We lived in the grayest city on earth

10 with a broom and a frazzled mop.
My daddy kept his passport in his pocket.
My daddy had a long eye and a manner of speaking.

Where are you from? people asked him.
He liked to tease. *I am from the land of stones.*

15 *I fell down from the tallest, oldest tree.*
In school, we were all from our own families.

I wanted a common name—Debbie, or Karen.
But the rest of it was good for me.

We had hummos,° pine nuts.

20   We had olive oil tipped from a shiny can.

Who wanted to go to the Methodist Church
or the neighborhood fish fry? We tried it all.
We didn't have to belong. Our parents took us seriously.
They took us everywhere they went.

25   Our days were studded with attention,
shadowed by twin cherry trees, thick.
We had umbrellas and boots.
We used good sense.

Our teachers said, Excuse me, how do you

30   pronounce this? Our teachers said, Welcome.
I don't know much about it, but tell me.
Do they still ride camels over there?

Whenever I think about the small white house,
our father is pitching sticks into a flaming barrel

35   in the backyard. It's as tall as I am. He sings as he stirs it.
His old country smelled like smoke.

What day can ever feel more real?
I'm linked to the jingling sound of keys
in someone else's pocket. I'm following behind.
I'll come in when they tell me to.

19. hummos (hum'əs): an appetizer made of mashed chickpeas, ground sesame seed paste, garlic, and other ingredients

Hugging the Jukebox

On an island the soft hue of memory,
moss green, kerosene yellow, drifting, mingling
in the Caribbean Sea,
a six-year-old named Alfred
5   learns all the words to all the songs
on his grandparents' jukebox, and sings them.
To learn the words is not so hard.
Many barmaids and teenagers have done as well.
But to sing as Alfred sings—
10   how can a giant whale live in the small pool of his chest?
How can there be breakers this high, notes crashing
at the beach of the throat,
and a reef of coral so enormous only the fishes know its size?

The grandparents watch. They can't sing.
15   They don't know who this voice is, trapped in their grandson's
        body.
They boy whose parents sent him back to the island
to chatter mango-talk and scrap with chickens—
at age three he didn't know the word "sad"!
Now he strings a hundred passionate sentences on a single
        line.
20   He bangs his fist so they will raise the volume.

What will they do together in their old age?
It is hard enough keeping yourself alive.
And this wild boy, loving nothing but music—
he'll sing all night, hugging the jukebox.
25   When a record pauses, that live second before dropping
        down,
  Alfred hugs tighter, arms stretched wide,

head pressed on the luminous belly. "Now!" he yells.
A half-smile when the needle breathes again.
They've tried putting him to bed, but he sings in bed.

30 Even in Spanish—and he doesn't speak Spanish!
Sings and screams, wants to go back to the jukebox.
O mama I was born with a trumpet in my throat
spent all these years tryin' to cough it up . . .

He can't even read yet. He can't *tell time.*
35 But he sings, and the chairs in this old dance hall jerk to
attention.
The grandparents lean on the counter, shaking their heads.
The customers stop talking and stare, goosey bumps surfacing
on their arms.
His voice carries out to the water where boats are tied
and sings for all of them, *a wave.*
40 For the hens, now roosting in trees,
for the mute boy next door, his second-best friend.
And for the hurricane, now brewing near Barbados—
a week forward neighbors will be hammering boards over
their windows,
rounding up dogs and fishing lines,
45 the generators will quit with solemn clicks in every yard.

But Alfred, hugging a sleeping jukebox, the names of the tunes
gone dark,
will still be singing, doubly loud now, teasing his grandmother,
"Put a coin in my mouth!" and believing what she wants to
believe;
this is not the end of the island, or the tablets this life has been
50 scribbled on, or the song.

What Brings Us Out

Something about pumpkins caused
the man who had not spoken in three years
to lean forward, cough, open his mouth.
How the room heaved into silence,
5   his words enormous in that air:
"I won't . . . be . . . afraid . . .
of my . . . father . . . anymore."
And what silence followed,
as if each heart had spoken
10   its most secret terror,
had combed the tangled clump
for the hardest line
and pulled it, intact,
from the mass.

15   I bless that man forever
for his courage, his voice
which started with one thing
and went to many, opening up and up
to the rim of the world.
20   So much silence had given him
a wisdom which held us all at bay,
amazed. Sometimes when I see
mountains of pumpkins by the roadside,
or watermelons, a hill of autumn gourds
25   piled lavishly on crates, I think
perhaps this one, or that, were it to
strike someone right,
this curl of hardened stalk,
this pleated skin . . .

30   or, on an old bureau drawer,
        the vegetable-like roundness of a glass knob
        that the baby turns and turns
        emerging, later, from a complicated dream . . .

        the huge navigational face of a radio
35   which never worked while I was alive
        but gave me more to go on than most sounds:
        how what brings us out may be
        small as that black arrow, swinging
        the wide arc, the numbers where silent voices lived,
40   how fast you had to turn to make it move.

The Lost Parrot

Carlos bites the end of his pencil
He's trying to write a dream-poem,
but waves at me, frowning

      I had a parrot

5   He talks slowly, like his voice travels far
to get out of his body

      A dream-parrot?
      No, a real parrot!
      Write about it

10   He squirms, looks nervous, everyone else
is almost finished and he hasn't started

      It left
      What left?
      The *parrot*

15   He hunches over the table, pencil gripped
in fist, shaping the heavy letters
Days later we will write story-poems, sound-poems,
but always the same subject for Carlos

      It left

20   He will insist on reading it and the class will look puzzled
The class is tired of the parrot

      Write more, Carlos
      I can't

      Why not?

25   I don't know   where   it went

Each day when I leave he stares at the ceiling
Maybe he is planning an expedition
into the back streets of San Antonio
armed with nets and ripe mangoes

30 He will find the parrot nesting in a rain gutter
This time he will guard it carefully, make sure it stays

Before winter comes and his paper goes white
in all directions

Before anything else he loves

35 gets away

So Far

notices   flutter
      from   telephone   poles
      until they   fade

OUR SWEET TABBY   AFRAID OF EVERYTHING
5   BIG GRAY CAT   HE IS OUR ONLY CHILD
SIBERIAN HUSKY   NEEDS HIS MEDICINE
FEMALE SCHNAUZER   WE ARE SICK WITH WORRY

    all night I imagine their feet
      tapping up the sidewalk
10   under the blooming crepe myrtle
      and the swoon of jasmine
        into the secret hedges
          into the dark cool caves
      of the banana-palm grove
15   and we cannot catch them
    or know what they are thinking
when they go so far from home

OUR BELOVED TURTLE   RED DOT ON FOREHEAD
VEGETARIAN   NAME OF KALI

20   please   please   please
    if you see them
call me   call me   call me

Poetry Paints a Picture

Poets can paint without a brush, sketch without a pencil, and create dazzling special effects without a Hollywood studio. Poets use words to create images, or pictures, in our minds. They want us to "see" the world they have created by appealing to our imaginations. In "Sleeping Father," one of the poems in this section, you will see, in your mind's eye, an old man snoring away in his chair. You will also see that man's dream of a kite and a long-lost village.

Often **poetic imagery** appeals to our sense of sight, but poets also stir our senses of hearing, touch, or even taste and smell. In "Juke Box Love Song," Langston Hughes conjures the many exciting sounds of Harlem—the growl and rumble of traffic and a juke box record. Stanley Kunitz makes us feel the slap on the cheek he received as a child over half a century ago. Janice Mirikitani evokes the taste of the strawberries her father grew and sold to white families but did not allow his own children to eat. Because we can sense the poets' worlds so vividly, we can also appreciate the emotions that drive their poems. We can share Hughes's love, Kunitz's grief, or Mirikitani's awe as her father refuses to give his children the sweet strawberries he grows in the desert.

Poets can make their images memorable by using **figurative language,** which includes figures of speech. A **figure of speech** compares two things that are basically not similar, but that have at least one surprising feature in common. In this chapter you will learn about various kinds of figurative language—similes, metaphors, personification, symbols, and allusions. We often use figures of speech in our daily language without thinking about it. For instance, an expression like "She's a live wire" is a metaphor. Poets offer us fresh figures of speech. Through imagery and figures of speech, poets invite us into their worlds and leave us more alive and alert in our own.

SIV CEDERING (1939–   )

The Changeling

One day you see it so clearly.
You could not really be their child.
Your parents would know it,
if they could look inside you.
5   Despite what relatives say
about mother's nose or smile
or father's eyes and toes,
the mirror tells the truth;
you are different.

10   At first you try to hide the fact.
You are glad you have been taken in
and have a place to sleep,
and eat. But soon,
you no longer want their charity.
15   You see through their affection.
You hear the phony note
in the assurance that of course
you are theirs, of course
they love you. You know better.

20   You look for a likeness in the faces
of strangers. You search for kinship
in books. You look at maps
that can show you the way.
You definitely know you are not
25   meant to do what your mother does,
your father. Even your supposed siblings,
however friendly and familiar,
cannot understand what occupies

your heart. So you choose to sleep
30   under the bed or in the attic.
You wish you had been left
to be brought up by the wolves,
or that the floating city
will soon return to collect
35   its lost children. You want
your real parents to finally come,
clutching the worn and torn documents
from the orphanage, to embrace you
with tear-stained faces.

40   Meanwhile you wait,
preparing. You study
your chosen subject. You write
your poems. You feed
the original flame that burns
45   inside you, because you know
that is the only way
you will get to live the life
that is meant to be yours.

MEET THE *Poet*

SIV CEDERING

Siv (rhymes with "Steve") Cedering creates what she calls poetry sculptures—large outdoor constructions that include poems or pieces of poems. In one of her poetry collections, Cedering has illustrated her poems with photographs she has taken. A talented visual artist, she combines her writing gifts with her talents in photography, painting, and sculpture. She also composes music.

Cedering was born near the Arctic Circle in Oeverkalix, Sweden. She was fourteen years old when she and her family came to live in San Francisco. At home in both English and Swedish, she has written five children's books—about a pig—and two novels in

Swedish. Not only does Cedering write her own works, but she also translates the work of others.

Knowing all the arts at which Cedering excels, you will not be surprised at the rich detail that appeals to our senses in "The Changeling." As you read, notice the sounds and images that the words create in your mind. You might even imagine what a poetry sculpture surrounding this poem might look like. In most of Cedering's poetry, she uses *I;* that is, she writes in the first person. However, "The Changeling" is written in the second person. It uses *you* and *your* instead of *I* and *my*. Consider why Cedering chose to do this and how the poem would read if she had used *I* and *my*.

VIC COCCIMIGLIO (1953–   )

St. Francis° Speaks to Me at a Young Age

For hours I sat on our driveway beneath the dogwood tree. After spotting some chirping birds my older brother had shaken a branch, knocking a baby robin, soft as a pumpkin's flesh, out of an unprotected nest.

5   That featherless bird lay motionless on the cold concrete, closed eyes bulging beneath a tiny domed head. My father and brother exchanged glances, and when their eyes met my brother ran away. I knelt beside the bird, my face to the cement, but found no movement of breath.

10   When the mother robin returned to her nest she found one less mouth singing with emptiness. She chirped and chirped at me; and all that day I sat beneath the dogwood tree, trying to explain my brother's action, something he has long forgotten, something I still don't understand.

° **St. Francis:** the patron saint of birds.

MEET THE *Poet*

VIC COCCIMIGLIO

"As a child I repeated words that fascinated me over and over, sometimes making them into silly songs. One day after church, my father said, 'Will you please stop that noise? Are you an *imbecile*?'"

"I thought: Am I a what? an *imbecile*. Bingo! I had a new word for the week."

"When I was growing up in Pittsburgh, Pennsylvania in the 1960s, words made a lasting impression on me. From an early age I loved the names of the city's three rivers: Allegheny, Monongahela, and Ohio. Dr. Morrow, our white-haired dentist who wore wire-rimmed glasses, told me that I had a *cavity* and he had to give me a shot of *Novocain,* which gave me a rhyme with *pain*. Bob Prince, radio station KDKA's colorful play-by-play announcer for the Pirates baseball team, referred to an incredibly high pop-up as 'a homerun in an elevator shaft.' A controversial play was 'closer than fuzz on a tic's ear.'"

"Once a fascinating word touches your heart and mind, you remember that day for the rest of your life—even if you are an imbecile. . . ."

Vic Coccimiglio was five years old when he had the experience that inspired him to write "St. Francis Speaks to Me at a Young Age." Now, as an adult, Vic continues to work at understanding his place in the world through his writing. His poems are paths to spiritual understanding.

DAVID CHIN (1953–   )

Sleeping Father

My father sits in his chair and snores.
Inhaling, he rasps like an anchor chain
rattling off a ship, dropping into the sea.
When he exhales, waves hiss on distant shores.

5   In his dream, he carries the kite
his uncle made for him and walks the village path
thinking of his father who sailed for America years ago.
I wonder if it has to be this way with fathers.

As he sleeps with his head tipped back,
10   his mouth half open, behind shut eyelids
the frailest of objects climbs the sky
and a string slides through his fingers.

MEET THE *Poet*

DAVID CHIN

David Chin discovered the magic of poetry in the liner notes for Bob Dylan's music albums. Chin particularly liked what Dylan had to say and how he said it in the lyrics of his songs. Chin discovered that the words to the songs, when written down, were poems.

Chin had actually started writing poetry when he was around eleven years old—only he didn't call what he wrote poems. At the time he thought of his work as simply doodling, sketching, and reacting in words to his experiences during the day and to the complicated rules of his New Jersey public school, which puzzled and annoyed him.

Chin pursued his discovery of poetry while he was in college and now teaches creative writing and literature. As you read "Sleeping Father," imagine that it is a song lyric. What sort of music might accompany these words?

JANICE MIRIKITANI (1941–   )

For My Father

He came over the ocean
carrying Mt. Fuji°
on his back / Tule Lake° on his chest
hacked through the brush
5   of deserts
and made them grow
strawberries

    we stole berries
    from the stem
10   we could not afford them
    for breakfast

his eyes held
nothing
as he whipped us
15   for stealing.
the desert had dried
his soul.

wordless
he sold
20   the rich,
full berries
to hakujines°
whose children
pointed at our eyes

2. **Mount Fuji:** a dormant volcano in Japan, considered sacred by many Japanese; often used
   as a symbol for Japan itself.
3. **Tule Lake** (to͞o′lē lāk): one of the internment camps where Japanese Americans were sent
   at the start of World War II.
22. **hakujines** (hä•ko͞o•jē′nās): Japanese word for white people.

25   they ate fresh
          strawberries
          with cream.

          Father,
          I wanted to scream
30   at your silence.
          Your strength
          was a stranger
          I could never touch.

          iron
35   in your eyes
          to shield
          the pain
          to shield desert-like wind
          from patches
40   of strawberries
          grown
          from
          tears.

MEET THE *Poet*

JANICE MIRIKITANI

Janice Mirikitani was just a baby in 1942. Unfortunately, because her family was Japanese American, they were sent to an internment camp in Arkansas. They, and many other Japanese Americans, had to give up their homes and possessions when they were interred in the camps during World War II. There they were under the constant watch and discipline of the camp officials.

Perhaps it was this early experience that motivated Mirikitani to take up her life work. Mirikitani is not only a poet; she has also spent almost four decades working for a church in San Francisco, helping to set up and run a number of programs that help those

in need of food, shelter, counseling, and jobs. Mirikitani also finds time to create dances for two dance groups and organize civil rights marches and demonstrations. She has received awards for all of these activities—her community service and her poetry.

The goal of much of Mirikitani's work is to lessen poverty in the world, to assist people who cannot live the lives they would like because they are poor. As you read "For My Father," think about how poverty affects the speaker in the poem, the father, and his family.

ANDREW HUDGINS (1951–   )

Tree

I'd like to be a tree. My father clinked
his fork down on his plate and stared at me.
"Boy, sometimes you say the dumbest things."
You ought to know, I muttered, and got backhanded
5   out of my chair. Nowdays, when I chop wood
and my hands gum with resin and bark flakes,
I hunker at the tap and wash them human.
But in math class, I'd daydream of my choices:
not hickory or cedar, not an oak—
10 post, red, live, pin, or water oak. Just pine.
If not longleaf, I'd settle for loblolly.
My skin would thicken with harsh bark, my limbs
sprout twigs, my twigs sprout elegant green needles.
Too soon, Miz Gorrie'd call on me. "Why did
15 you do step four that way?" *Who me? Step four?*
"Yes, Andrew, you. Step four." *Beats me. It looked
good at the time, I guess*—and got invited
to come back after school and guess again.
And that's when I decided it: scrub pine.

The Air

Because I'd seen a man
thrust his straight fingers through
a melon, I spent childhood
stalking a long hall, punching
5   the air in front of me.
Punch where your throat would be!
Kick where your crotch would be!
the sensei° yelled. I grunted,
screamed fiercely, and snapped my fists,
10   driving them through the soft parts
of the me that wasn't there.
I punched pure air and tried
to shatter it—the air,
which simply opened, fell back,
15   gave way as my hands slashed through.
The air! I can't believe
how much I hated it.

---

8. **sensei** (sen'sā): the respectful title for an instructor or teacher in Japan; a martial arts
instructor in the U.S.

Childhood of the Ancients

Hard? You don't know what hard is, boy:
When I was your age we got up in pitch dark,
and walked five miles to school and ten miles back,
uphill both ways, and all we had for lunch
5   was a cold sweet potato and dry cornbread.
And when we got back home your grandma made us
chop cotton, slop the hogs, then milk the chickens
before supper, and all we had to eat
was chicken-fried pine straw and redeye gravy.
10   Maybe some turnip greens. Maybe some collards.
But what do you know? Shoot, you've always had
hot food plopped in front of you, like magic.
For you, it's all ice cream and soda pop.

MEET THE *Poet*

ANDREW HUDGINS

When Andrew Hudgins was young, he noticed the books that he liked to read had something missing: the anger, bewilderment, and sense of powerlessness that children often feel at home, at school, or among their friends. People usually avoid speaking of these experiences, but Hudgins decided as a boy that they should be given voice, and that if he ever wrote about his childhood, he would record them.

Hudgins was born in Killeen, Texas, but because his father was in the United States Air Force, the family moved often. Although cities, schools, and friends came and went during his childhood, his books were always with him. Like many other readers, he enjoyed escaping into a good book, pretending to be the book's hero, living a bold and exciting life.

Hudgins taught elementary school for a short time, but what he really wanted to do was write. He worked at various jobs and continued his education while he learned his craft. His first books of poetry, about the American South and its history, were successful.

"Tree," "The Air," and "Childhood of the Ancients" describe the emotions Hudgins felt as a young boy. As you read them, you will see that Hudgins deals with these serious feelings with a touch of humor.

LI-YOUNG LEE (1957–   )

I Ask My Mother to Sing

She begins, and my grandmother joins her.
Mother and daughter sing like young girls.
If my father were alive, he would play
his accordion and sway like a boat.

5   I've never been in Peking, or the Summer Palace,
nor stood on the great Stone Boat to watch
the rain begin on Kuen Ming Lake, the picnickers
running away in the grass.

But I love to hear it sung;
10   how the waterlilies fill with rain until
they overturn, spilling water into water,
then rock back, and fill with more.

Both women have begun to cry.
But neither stops her song.

MEET THE *Poet*

LI-YOUNG LEE

Not many poets writing in America today can claim royal blood. However, Li-Young Lee is definitely royal—his mother was a member of the Chinese royal family, and his mother's grandfather was the first president of the Republic of China. However, the family had to flee persecution in China and was living in Indonesia when Lee was born. Eventually, Lee's father, who was a doctor in China, brought his family to the United States and became pastor of a small church in Pennsylvania.

Lee's father read to his children from the King James version of the Bible and quoted from the three hundred Chinese poems he had memorized. As a child, Lee was enchanted by the poetry and stories, but it seemed to him that only angels or long-dead poets wrote poems. Not until he was a college student did he realize that living human beings—people of all sorts—write poetry. It was then that Lee began to write poems about his own experiences.

Lee's family all live together because, as a family, they feel dislocated. Their land and possessions in China no longer belong to them, and Lee often feels disconnected from any place that he can call home. This is the reason he writes of the past—to keep the family's memories alive and to understand their stories.

STANLEY KUNITZ (1905–   )

The Portrait

My mother never forgave my father
for killing himself,
especially at such an awkward time
and in a public park,

5   that spring
when I was waiting to be born.
She locked his name
in her deepest cabinet
and would not let him out,

10   though I could hear him thumping.
When I came down from the attic
with the pastel portrait in my hand
of a long lipped stranger
with a brave moustache

15   and deep brown level eyes,
she ripped it into shreds
without a single word
and slapped me hard.
In my sixty-fourth year

20   I can feel my cheek
still burning.

MEET THE *Poet*

STANLEY KUNITZ

As a child, Stanley Kunitz would trek into the woods behind his house and yell words, especially big, complicated words, just to hear their powerful, mysterious sounds. He treasured the family dictionary for its inexhaustible supply of new and interesting words. Now in his nineties, Kunitz is still writing poetry, and the sound of words still intrigues him. Poetry, he advises, is meant to be read aloud. After all, poetry started out as song and dance, and when poetry moves away from this to become a highly technical skill, people will stop listening to it. Kunitz says that he does not write poetry so much as speak it to himself.

Kunitz felt the call of poetry when he was very young. He never claims that writing poetry is easy, however: It is hard work that requires time alone, time to think about ways to arrange words that will be new and fresh for readers. Sometimes, he says, a poem that fits nicely onto a single page may take months to write. Kunitz believes that gardening and writing poetry are much alike. In each case, one must prune away every weed, or every unneeded word, until what remains is beautiful.

Kunitz says that poetry is about storytelling, and in "The Portrait" he tells a dramatic story from his childhood, recollected many years later.

LANGSTON HUGHES (1902–1967)

Juke Box Love Song

I could take the Harlem night
and wrap around you,
Take the neon lights and make a crown,
Take the Lenox Avenue buses,
5   Taxis, subways,
And for your love song tone their rumble down.
Take Harlem's heartbeat,
Make a drumbeat,
Put it on a record, let it whirl,
10   And while we listen to it play,
Dance with you till day—
Dance with you, my sweet brown Harlem girl.

MEET THE *Poet*

LANGSTON HUGHES

Langston Hughes was a twenty-three-year-old busboy at a hotel in Washington, D.C., collecting the dirty dishes from the restaurant tables, when he saw a chance to have his poetry read by a famous poet, Vachel Lindsay. Hughes quietly placed three of his poems on the table beside Lindsay's plate and hurried back to the kitchen. At a poetry reading held that night, Lindsay announced that there was another poet at the hotel and read Hughes's poems. The resulting publicity was a great help to Hughes, who had just signed a contract to have his first collection of poetry published.

Hughes was very different from other poets of his time: He decided to tie his poetry to the ordinary speech of African Americans. He also incorporated the rhythms and cadences of jazz and the blues in his work. Hughes wrote of everyday African Americans living ordinary lives. His poems tell of the days and nights of working-class people in Harlem and other cities. He was criticized by people who thought his poetry should be written about more heroic or more intellectual aspects of African American subjects. Nevertheless, he continued to champion everyday people, writing about them in everyday language; and they enthusiastically supported his work.

GWENDOLYN BROOKS (1917–2000)

the sonnet-ballad

Oh mother, mother, where is happiness?
They took my lover's tallness off to war,
Left me lamenting. Now I cannot guess
What I can use an empty heart-cup for.

5   He won't be coming back here any more.
Some day the war will end, but, oh, I knew
When he went walking grandly out that door
That my sweet love would have to be untrue.
Would have to be untrue. Would have to court

10   Coquettish° death, whose impudent and strange
Possessive arms and beauty (of a sort)
Can make a hard man hesitate—and change.
And he will be the one to stammer, "Yes."
Oh mother, mother, where is happiness?

---

10. coquettish (kō•ket'ish): flirtatious.

MEET THE *Poet*

GWENDOLYN BROOKS

Everyone loves to win a prize. Gwendolyn Brooks was awarded one of the most distinguished prizes in the United States, the Pulitzer Prize in poetry, when she was thirty-three years old. She was the first African American author to win that prize. However, Brooks went on to win many other prizes during her long career as a poet and author. She once wrote that most people like "tidy answers"; but she turned her attention to "all the little ravelings" that were usually ignored by others and wrote of the ways ordinary African Americans lived in the city.

Later in her life, Brooks used her influence to encourage African American writers by assisting new African American publishing companies. She went on to become Poetry Consultant to the Library of Congress, the first African American woman to hold that post. She visited schools, universities, hospitals, and prisons to read poetry and to encourage poets. By the time of her death, Brooks had received approximately fifty honorary degrees and was known internationally.

CHRISTIAN LANGWORTHY
(1967–   )

Mango

You put the mango in the clay jar,
bury it in rice. In the days that pass
you hope it will ripen. Your
mother has told you not to

5   lift the lid too soon, or
the mango will remain green.
You sweep away dust from the corner
where the jar sits like a shrine.
Now and then, you put your hand over

10   the clay lid and count the days gone by.

Monsoon season has passed. Men of war
had asked you questions and left with
their mysteries unsolved. You remember
your father in his pressed uniform,

15   the face of an American soldier,
followed by countless others who
handed you gum and patted your shoulder.

In the corner, the rice jar sits—the mango
deep inside. All the time, you wonder:

20   When will it be ripe? The sun bakes
the sidewalks. You learn to ignore
the pain of walking on hot cement.
From off the street, behind a screen door,
someone sees your face and spits at the dust.

25 They know who you are. They have a name for
    your kind, you child of the dust.

    In the one-room house, all you have left are
    cloths and shelter, your mother and the mango.
    The dust has settled. Day and night you wonder
30 how the mango will look after the days gone by.
    You take the mango out of the jar
    to see if it has ripened and wipe away
    the rice dust that dulls the color
    of a fruit once green and untouched.

MEET THE *Poet*

CHRISTIAN LANGWORTHY

Christian Langworthy knows how to capture an everyday experience and make it a memorable poem.

Langworthy was born in Vietnam. His mother was Vietnamese, and his father was an American soldier. Langworthy and his brother were rejected by the people in Da Nang where they lived, partly because of their mixed parentage. Neither boy ever knew his father; their mother told the boys that their fathers were dead.

Langworthy and his brother were fascinated by the American soldiers in Da Nang. They played at being soldiers and wanted to

believe that they were sons of two of these men in uniform. They collected castoff army gear—dented canteens, spent shells, and even live rounds of ammunition. Sometimes the soldiers gave them presents and treats like gum and candy.

When he was seven years old, Langworthy's life changed dramatically. He was given up by his mother and airlifted out of Saigon as part of a "baby lift," in which orphan children were brought to the United States to be adopted. With new parents and a new environment, Vietnam and Langworthy's life there was pushed into the background. When he went to college, Langworthy began to look back on that life. "Mango" is a result of that looking back.

JUDITH ORTIZ COFER (1952–   )

My Grandfather's Hat

in memory of Basiliso Morot Cordero

I cannot stop thinking of that old hat
he is wearing in the grave: the last gift
of love from his wife before they fell
into the habit of silence.

5   Forgotten as the daughters chose
the funeral clothes, it sat
on his dresser as it always had:
old leather, aromatic of his individual self,
pliable as an old companion, ready to go

10   anywhere with him.

The youngest grandchild remembered
and ran after her father, who was carrying
the old man's vanilla suit—the one worn to bodas,
bautismos, and elections—like a lifeless

15   child in his arms: *No te olvides*
del sombrero de abuelo.

I had seen him hold the old hat in his lap
and caress it as he talked of the good times,
and when he walked outside, place it on his head

20   like a blessing.

My grandfather, who believed in God,
the Gracious Host, Proprietor of the Largest Hacienda.
May it be so. May heaven
be an island in the sun,

25   where a good man may wear his hat with pride,
glad that he could take it with him.

MEET THE *Poet*

JUDITH ORTIZ COFER

When she was a child, Judith Ortiz Cofer's family alternated between living in Puerto Rico and New Jersey, and she felt that she didn't belong, no matter where she lived. When Cofer's family lived in Puerto Rico, she was part of her mother's extended family, even though she was accused of sounding like a "gringa" when she spoke Spanish. There Cofer listened to her grandmother's stories, free in the tropical surroundings of Puerto Rico and at one with the rich gifts of nature. When Cofer's father moved the family to New Jersey, she was made fun of for her Spanish accent. In the cold, northern city where she lived, she became an avid watcher of television. She also read for hours on end and developed a passion for fairy tales.

In many ways, Cofer may have felt she could not win. However, Cofer did win. She has become a poet and author whose writing forms a bridge between the two worlds of her childhood—warm, tropical Puerto Rico and a cold, northern city. Cofer has also won in a way that is particularly important for young people—she has taken her feelings and experiences, such as the feeling of being left out, and written about them. She believes that people of any age can do this and learn to understand themselves and their world.

YUSEF KOMUNYAKAA (1947–   )

Banking Potatoes

Daddy would drop purple-veined vines
Along rows of dark loam
& I'd march behind him
Like a peg-legged soldier,
5   Pushing down the stick
With a V cut into its tip.

Three weeks before the first frost
I'd follow his horse-drawn plow
That opened up the soil & left
10   Sweet potatoes sticky with sap,
Like flesh-colored stones along a riverbed
Or diminished souls beside a mass grave.

Facing It

My black face fades,
hiding inside the black granite.
I said I wouldn't,
dammit: No tears.
5   I'm stone. I'm flesh.
My clouded reflection eyes me
like a bird of prey, the profile of night
slanted against morning. I turn
this way—the stone lets me go.
10   I turn that way—I'm inside
the Vietnam Veterans Memorial°
again, depending on the light
to make a difference.
I go down the 58,022 names,
15   half-expecting to find
my own in letters like smoke.
I touch the name Andrew Johnson;
I see the booby trap's white flash.
Names shimmer on a woman's blouse
20   but when she walks away
the names stay on the wall.
Brushstrokes flash, a red bird's
wings cutting across my stare.
The sky. A plane in the sky.
25   A white vet's image floats

---

11. Vietnam Veterans Memorial: in Washington, D.C.

closer to me, then his pale eyes
look through mine. I'm a window.
He's lost his right arm
inside the stone. In the black mirror
30   a woman's trying to erase names:
No, she's brushing a boy's hair.

MEET THE *Poet*

YUSEF KOMUNYAKAA

Yusef Komunyakaa's family name originates with his grandfather who probably stowed away on a ship that sailed to the United States from Trinidad. He arrived wearing one boy's shoe and one girl's shoe—a bizarre fact that Komunyakaa wrote about in a poem called "Mismatched Shoes."

Komunyakaa, an African American, grew up in the deep South in Louisiana. His mother encouraged him to read and bought him a set of encyclopedias. At the age of sixteen, Komunyakaa read a book of essays by James Baldwin, a famous African American writer, and was inspired to write.

However, before Komunyakaa began his university education, he went to Vietnam and served in the military, winning a bronze star. Komunyakaa began to write poetry after his return from Vietnam, while he was studying at the University of Colorado.

Komunyakaa uses simple, forceful language in short lines that are at once easy to read and packed with ideas and images. His poems about Vietnam have gathered special praise; they tell the stories not only of the soldiers who served in the war but also of the people who waited in the States, watching the news on TV.

JOHN HAINES (1924–   )

If the Owl Calls Again

At dusk
from the island in the river
and it's not too cold,

I'll wait for the moon
5   to rise,

then take wing and glide
to meet him.

We will not speak,
but hooded against the frost
10   soar above
the alder flats, searching
with tawny eyes.

And then we'll sit
in the shadowy spruce and
15   pick the bones
of careless mice,
while the long moon drifts
toward Asia
and the river mutters
20   in its icy bed.

And when morning climbs
the limbs
we'll part without a sound,

fulfilled, floating
25   homeward as
the cold world awakens.

Wolves

Last night I heard wolves howling,
their voices coming from afar
over the wind-polished ice—so much
brave solitude in that sound.

5   They are death's snowbound sailors;
they know only a continual
drifting between moonlit islands,
their tongues licking the stars.

But they sing as good seamen should,
10   and tomorrow the sun will find them,
yawning and blinking
the snow from their eyelashes.

Their voices rang through the frozen
water of my human sleep,
15   blown by the night wind
with the moon for an icy sail.

MEET THE *Poet*

JOHN HAINES

The images you find in John Haines's poems may make you shiver. He writes of a frozen, white landscape in which humans are not important. He describes the owl gliding from the island in the river and the wolves howling in the night—describes them so vividly that we can see the owl winging across the water and hear the wolves calling to one another.

Haines is an artist as well as a poet. He uses his sense of color to create powerful images of the frozen Alaskan landscape.

Haines is also a nature poet, making the natural world the main subject of his poetry. He has spent much of his life outdoors fishing, hunting, and trapping for a living in Alaska. Later, he homesteaded there, settling on a tract of land. When Haines was not busy earning his living, he had long stretches of quiet time in which to think about the land and its stillness, about the animals that manage to live and even thrive there, and about the role of people in nature. Haines continues to live and write in Alaska. He is presently working on an autobiography, in which he tells about his years of homesteading, as well as about the history of the area where he lives.

TED KOOSER

You might think that a Midwestern life insurance executive—
which is what Ted Kooser was—would be plain and predictable. As
a poet, Kooser writes about the everyday events that you yourself
experience and know. You, too, have seen old dogs move around in
a home. You know that people often turn thoughtful at the end of
a weekend, a season, or a year.

However, don't be taken in by the ordinariness of the themes
and situations in Kooser's poetry. Kooser is a master of the artful
and subtle surprise.

Look at "First Snow," for example. Kooser
packs the first eight lines with familiar images
and sayings. For people who live in cold
climates, a few bright, white flakes on a black
surface—of a dog, a car, or pavement—signal
that the first snow is coming. Kooser shows how
his fellow Midwesterners typically greet that
first snow. They gather in the kitchen and talk
about the fact that every snowflake is different
or recall a colder, heavier snowfall.

From a poetic point of view, what these
people say is quite ordinary; only a little child
would think them exciting or original. Right in
the middle of the poem, however, Kooser surprises you with an
amusing metaphor, likening the kitchen to a kindergarten. You
suddenly see that all the folks in the kitchen, young or old, are
rekindling the sense of wonder they felt as five-year-olds, learning
for the first time that every flake has a unique shape. Kooser
describes the old dog retiring for the evening, and then he delivers
his grand surprise. As he describes the approach of evening, we
suddenly picture it as a dark, affectionate, slow-moving dog, made

brilliant by the diamond snow. Within the world of the poem, a familiar image of a beloved old pet has become a fresh, new metaphor for a winter's night.

Kooser's "Selecting a Reader," however, contains another kind of surprise. Whether they admit it or not, poets tend to fantasize about their readers, just as readers fantasize or wonder about the poets. In the first seven lines of "Selecting a Reader," Kooser begins building an image of the kind of reader that you might expect him to dream about. She is beautiful, and she approaches his book in a sensitive and solitary manner that seems fitting for a poetry fan. Kooser adds a particular, tender detail to this general picture: The reader's hair is still damp, as if she could not wait to get to the bookstore to check out his poetry.

However, the next detail is unexpected. The beautiful woman wears an old raincoat that she cannot afford to have cleaned. You may take a nanosecond to adjust to this unromantic image, but Kooser is not through surprising us. You may think this grubby reader would adore the poet's book, buy all the copies on the shelf, and order more for her friends. Not so. In the last lines you discover that you have been set up. Kooser gets the better of us and our routine expectations, and the poem gets the better of poets, and their vanity.

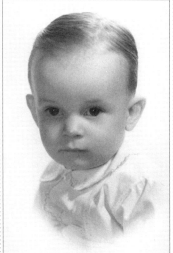

Kooser writes about ordinary things, seeing his work as a poet as giving us knowledge of the ordinary world in ways we have never known before. Kooser's world may seem at first unglamorous and ordinary, but through artful surprise, the poet transforms it into a world that dazzles the senses and keeps artistic egos modest.

TED KOOSER (1939–   )

First Snow

The old black dog comes in one evening
with the first few snowflakes on his back
and falls asleep, throwing his bad leg out
at our excitement. This is the night
5   when one of us gets to say, as if it were news,
that no two snowflakes are ever alike;
the night when each of us remembers something
snowier. The kitchen is a kindergarten
steamy with stories. The dog gets stiffly up
10   and limps away, seeking a quiet spot
at the heart of the house. Outside,
in silence, with diamonds in his fur,
the winter night curls round the legs of the trees,
sleepily blinking snowflakes from his lashes.

At the End of the Weekend

It is Sunday afternoon,
and I suddenly miss
my distant son, who at ten
has just this instant buzzed
5   my house in a flying
cardboard box, dipping
one wing to look down over
my shimmering roof, the yard,
the car in the drive. In his room
10   three hundred miles from me,
he tightens his helmet,
grips the controls, turns
loops and rolls. My windows
rattle. On days like this,
15   the least quick shadow crossing
the page makes me look up
at the sky like a goose,
squinting to see that flash
that I dream is his thought of me
20   daring to fall through the distance,
then climbing, full throttle, away.

Selecting a Reader

First, I would have her be beautiful,
and walking carefully up on my poetry
at the loneliest moment of an afternoon,
her hair still damp at the neck
5 from washing it. She should be wearing
a raincoat, an old one, dirty
from not having money enough for the cleaners.
She will take out her glasses, and there
in the bookstore, she will thumb
10 over my poems, then put the book back
up on its shelf. She will say to herself,
"For that kind of money, I can get
my raincoat cleaned." And she will.

Flying at Night

Above us, stars. Beneath us, constellations.
Five billion miles away, a galaxy dies
like a snowflake falling on water. Below us,
some farmer, feeling the chill of that distant death,
5   snaps on his yard light, drawing his sheds and barn
back into the little system of his care.
All night, the cities, like shimmering novas,
tug with bright streets at lonely lights like his.

Year's End

Now the seasons are closing their files
on each of us, the heavy drawers
full of certificates rolling back
into the tree trunks, a few old papers
5   flocking away. Someone we loved
has fallen from our thoughts,
making a little, glittering splash
like a bicycle pushed by a breeze.
Otherwise, not much has happened;
10   we fell in love again, finding
that one red feather on the wind.

Messages

Every poem in this anthology carries a message. This is, after all, one of the reasons we read poetry—to find out what a particular poet or a specific poem has to say about its subject.

Because a poem is written in language that is more condensed and also more intense than ordinary language, it may take you a bit of practice to get the message. Sometimes the poet helps out and makes his or her message clear and open—often stating it at the end of the poem. Some of the poets in this section have used this technique. Other poets hide their message using sound, images, and figures of speech, and you have to work at discovering these to figure out the message. The message you receive may not be the same as that received by others. This is because, in the end, a poem is a very personal communication between the poet and the reader.

A clue to the message of a poem is its **tone**. This is the poet's attitude toward the subject of the poem. It is usually suggested rather than stated outright. Tone can usually be stated in one word. For example, some poems are humorous. Others are serious, or angry, or sad. A poem could describe happy events from a poet's childhood, but the attitude of the poet toward these events may be resentment or fear. This is revealed by the speaker's **tone**.

The words the poet chooses signal the tone. If a poet describes a person as scrawny rather than slender, the tone is critical or sarcastic. The comparisons a poet makes also reveal tone. Comparing a singer's voice to the sound of a flute is very different from comparing that voice to the cawing of a crow. Other ways poets convey tone is through rhythm and rhyme. A brisk, jazzy rhythm gives you a much different impression than a slow, solemn beat.

In the poems that follow, each poet has a message for you. Take the time to receive the message.

NIKKI GIOVANNI (1943–   )

Nikki-Rosa

Childhood remembrances are always a drag
if you're Black
you always remember things like living in Woodlawn
with no inside toilet
5 and if you become famous or something
they never talk about how happy you were to have your
        mother
all to yourself and
how good the water felt when you got your bath from one of
        those
big tubs that folk in Chicago barbecue in
10 and somehow when you talk about home
it never gets across how much you
understood their feelings
as the whole family attended meetings about Hollydale
and even though you remember
15 your biographers never understand
your father's pain as he sells his stock
and another dream goes
and though you're poor it isn't poverty that
concerns you
20 and though they fought a lot
it isn't your father's drinking that makes any difference
but only that everybody is together and you
and your sister have happy birthdays and very good
        christmases
and I really hope no white person ever has cause to write
        about me

25   because they never understand Black love is Black wealth and
          they'll
      probably talk about my hard childhood and never understand
          that
      all the while I was quite happy

MEET THE *Poet*

NIKKI GIOVANNI

"I come from a long line of storytellers," Nikki Giovanni replies when asked how she became a poet. Giovanni's grandfather told the myths that he had read while studying Latin, and her mother told the stories that she loved. Giovanni's outspoken grandmother greatly influenced her granddaughter by telling Giovanni about her African American heritage. Years of listening to the voices of her family telling stories had a big impact on Giovanni. "I appreciated the quality and the rhythm of the telling of the stories," she once

commented. When Giovanni started to write, she worked hard to make her poems sound like someone speaking naturally. Perhaps Giovanni sums it up best when she says, "I want my writing to sound like I talk." What does Giovanni talk about in her poetry? She writes about what she sees around her, what she experiences, and what she knows.

Giovanni knows about racism firsthand. As a child in Knoxville, Tennessee, she was frightened by the violence that regularly occurred there. "You always felt someone was trying to kill you," she wrote in an autobiographical essay. Giovanni's early activist poems spoke out angrily against racial prejudice. At the same time, Giovanni wrote more personally expressive poetry about her childhood and her family. "Nikki-Rosa," is an example of this and has become Giovanni's most beloved and most published poem.

PAT MORA (1942–   )

Fences

Mouths full of laughter,
the *turistas* come to the tall hotel
with suitcases full of dollars.

Every morning my brother makes
5   the cool beach sand new for them.
With a wooden board he smooths
away all footprints.

I peek through the cactus fence
and watch the women rub oil
10   sweeter than honey into their arms and legs
while their children jump waves
or sip drinks from long straws,
coconut white, mango yellow.

Once my little sister
15   ran barefoot across the hot sand
for a taste.

My mother roared like the ocean,
"No. No. It's their beach.
It's their beach."

MEET THE *Poet*

PAT MORA

Mothers can be fierce defenders of their children and Pat Mora's mother is a good example of this. She and Mora's father made great financial sacrifices in order to give their children a good education. Mora's mother regularly took her children to the library and books became an important part of their lives. Mora's mother also encouraged her children to write and became her daughter's first editor. She continues to read everything written about her daughter as well as every word her daughter writes. Mora wrote a poem about her mother describing her as a woman who is afraid of no one and who refuses to be treated unfairly. She called it "My Fierce Mother."

It is no surprise that Mora should feel that a society that ignores the Mexican heritage of many of its people is unfair. At first, as a child growing up in El Paso, Texas, Mora tried to fit in. At home, she spoke Spanish with her family, but at school she conformed. This meant that she had to give up or ignore most of her Hispanic heritage. As an adult, Mora fiercely defends her right to write poetry that tells about all of her life and experience, believing that her words can help change society. "I take pride in being a Hispanic writer. I will continue to write and to struggle to say what no other writer can say in quite the same way."

LOUISE ERDRICH (1954–   )

I Was Sleeping Where the Black Oaks Move

We watched from the house
as the river grew, helpless
and terrible in its unfamiliar body.
Wrestling everything into it,
5   the water wrapped around trees
until their life-hold was broken.
They went down, one by one,
and the river dragged off their covering.

Nests of the herons, roots washed to bones,
10   snags of soaked bark on the shoreline:
a whole forest pulled through the teeth
of the spillway.° Trees surfacing
singly, where the river poured off
into arteries for fields below the reservation.

15   When at last it was over, the long removal,
they had all become the same dry wood.
We walked among them, the branches
whitening in the raw sun.
Above us drifted herons,
20   alone, hoarse-voiced, broken,
settling their beaks among the hollows.

Grandpa said, *These are the ghosts of the tree people,*
moving above us, unable to take their rest.

Sometimes now, we dream our way back to the heron dance.

---

12. spillway: a channel around a dam that carries away extra water.

25 Their long wings are bending the air
  into circles through which they fall.
  They rise again in shifting wheels.
  How long must we live in the broken figures
  their necks make, narrowing the sky.

30 Some nights in town's cold winter,
  earth shakes.
  People say it's a train full of danger
  or the plane-broken barriers of sound,
  but out there
35 behind the dark trunks of trees
  the gone elk have pulled the hide of earth
  tight and they are drumming
  back the woodland,
  tall grass and days we were equal
40 and strong.

MEET THE *Poet*

LOUISE ERDRICH

As a little girl, Louise Erdrich was encouraged to write. Her father gave her a nickel for every story she produced. Her mother wove strips of construction paper into covers and stapled the pages together to make a book. Erdrich tells us, "So at an early age I felt myself to be a published author earning substantial royalties."

Erdrich is a child of parents from two very different cultures—a German American father and a Chippewa Indian mother. Erdrich says that her interest in writing grew naturally as she listened to the stories of her family and other American Indian families in Wahpeton, North Dakota, where she grew up. " . . . when you grow up constantly hearing the stories rise, break, and fall, it gets into you somehow."

Her diverse heritage has given Erdrich her themes and characters. She is perhaps best known for a series of novels that tell the stories of three interrelated families who live either in or close to an American Indian reservation in North Dakota.

The mythic quality of American Indian storytelling is reflected in Erdrich's poetry. In "I Was Sleeping Where the Black Oaks Move" Erdrich tells much more than the story of a flood—it is the story of the destruction of living trees, the birds that lived in them, and the ghostly elk who bring back the woodland.

MARIA MAZZIOTTI GILLAN
(1940–   )

In New Jersey Once

In New Jersey once, marigolds grew wild.
Fields swayed with daisies.
Oaks stood tall on mountains.
Powdered butterflies graced the velvet air.

5   Listen. It was like that.
Before the bulldozers.
Before the cranes.
Before the cement sealed the earth.

Even the stars, which used to hang
10   in thick clusters in the black sky,
even the stars are dim.

Burrow under the blacktop,
under the cement, the old dark earth
is still there. Dig your hands into it,
15   feel it, deep, alive on your fingers.

Know that the earth breathes and pulses still.
Listen. It mourns. In New Jersey once, flowers grew.

MEET THE *Poet*

MARIA MAZZIOTTI GILLAN

Sometimes people feel that their everyday lives are just too ordinary to write about. Maria Mazziotti Gillan does not feel that way. Her poetry is about her life, her family, and her home.

Gillan loves the landscape of New Jersey. In her poem, "In New Jersey Once," she writes about the beauty of that landscape as it was in the past. Development seems to have destroyed that beauty, and the poet reminds us that the living earth is still there, mourning the loss of beauty.

Gillan feels that earlier American poets like Walt Whitman, William Carlos Williams, and Allen Ginsberg have influenced her writing. "I love to read and I've always read a great deal of poetry."

Being a first-generation Italian American, Gillan strongly identifies with immigrants and with those who do not have the ability to express themselves. She wants her poetry to provide a voice for these people.

Presently at work on a memoir, Gillan continues to use her life, the landscape, and voiceless people as the main focus of her writing.

INDRAN AMIRTHANAYAGAM (1960–)

The Elephants Are in the Yard

I see the elephants in the yard
Pappa, the white snake too
peering out of the neem° tree's trunk
hissing poisons

5   Pappa, I see the wild boar
in the thicket, the branches
burning with his smell, Pappa
bring out your gun,

I want to eat the boar's meat
10   and stare at his head
on my wall, Pappa I see
the elephants in the yard

The partridge and jungle fowl
you shot from the air and bush
15   to conquer alone
the harvest of the jungle

You were always a sport
took on bird in flight, boar
in fierce charge, your life or his
20   I see the elephants in the yard

and poachers° cock-eyed
devouring their tusks in dreams

---

3. **neem:** a tropical evergreen tree grown in Asia for its wood and fragrant oil.
21. **poachers:** trespassers who hunt animals unlawfully.

building grand compounds
massing riches in stainless steel

25   Pappa, the sport is finished
the elephants are in the yard
and there is no forest
and there are lots of knives

and forks and tractors
30   and babies to feed
and guerrillas hiding
in the shade of neem and mango

right there beyond the verandah,
in the center of the garden
35   where your dowry° will build
your last daughter's house

the elephants spread their heavy bodies
tired from the journey up country
and down country, the long herding
40   to some safe peaceful house.

35. dowry (dou'rē): wealth or property that a woman brings to her husband when she marries.

MEET THE *Poet*

INDRAN AMIRTHANAYAGAM

Indran Amirthanayagam is a man on the move. He was born on the island of Sri Lanka, located in the Indian Ocean near the southern tip of India. When he was eight, his family moved to London. Later, the family moved yet again, this time to the United States. Amirthanayagam has served with the United States Foreign Service in Mexico City, in Belgium, and is now in India.

"When I was a boy I lived in Ceylon, now called Sri Lanka. I used to hunt with my grandfather. This was one of my principal pleasures: the mystery of the jungle, the sounds of birds, the rustle of snakes and lizards, the tremendous force of a charging elephant—and the quiet and serene calm of seeing elephants at play in a stream."

"The elephant lives in herds, in families. An elephant may live sixty or seventy years if allowed to age without fear of a gun or knife or poison. Sometimes an elephant is kicked out of its herd and becomes a rogue, wandering alone in the jungle."

Amirthanayagam uses the elephant as a symbol in his poetry. In "The Elephants Are in the Yard," Amirthanayagam tells us that he is using the elephant herd and the expelled rogue elephant to describe the civil war in his country. "The multi-ethnic family of Sri Lanka—composed of Sinhalese, Tamils, Muslims, Burghers—suddenly got rid of one family member—the Tamil. This sparked a declaration of independence and a struggle for a separate Tamil homeland."

Amirthanayagam, a Tamil, also uses the elephant as a symbol for what is best in ourselves—the best that we can be. This, of course, includes hope for our future. "I go back to my homeland as an adult and there are, of course, members of my family—cousins, uncles—living contentedly. In "The Elephants Are in the Yard," I say there is no forest, and I speak of the dowry that will build your last daughter's house. However, the daughter has given birth to a daughter and there is still some forest left. In the larger multi-ethnic family of Sri Lanka, perhaps peace will be found again with some settlement of the Tamil concerns."

Amirthanayagam is still a man on the move.

ROSEMARY CATACALOS
(1944–   )

Morning Geography

Suppose the flower rioting on my desk, an exotic shout of
    yellow
streaked with red and ruffled like an agitated jungle bird,

suppose this flower, large as my hand, could be pulled apart
and the sweetness wrung out the way we did honeysuckle
    so long

5   ago on heavy summer nights with fireflies: *This drop of
    honey*
*for courage, this drop of honey for love, this drop for
    anything*

you are dreaming of . . . Last night I dreamed a woman I love
(in Spanish we say *dreamed* with, *soñe* con *Noemi*) running
    furiously

through Texas sagebrush to save her Uncle Mohammed,
    who died
10   on a mountain in Palestine years ago, a hermit who wanted
    no saving.

Dreams are like this, make all things possible. The way just
    now,
still drugged with sleep, I supposed a loud flower could save
    us, tell us

something about sweetness when half a world away a man
    tends a fire
in the street before his tiny rug shop, a short distance from
    some broken

15   buildings. He breathes the dense smoke of burning rubber,
        tires
    to make the bombers think they've already struck here.
        Suppose we could

    have coffee with him, strong, laced with cardamom° and
        small talk.
    Suppose we'd figured out, on those immense and long
        ago

    lost summer nights, how to get at the sweetness
20   without tearing the proud throat of even one blossom.

17. cardamom (kär′də•məm): aromatic spice belonging to the ginger family.

MEET THE *Poet*

ROSEMARY CATACALOS

"I began writing poems as a small child, though I didn't call it that at first. As far as I knew, I simply told myself stories. From a very young age, I was left alone or with relatives while my parents worked, or I worked alongside them. It was a hard and angry life, and I didn't feel I belonged anywhere—home, church, school—nowhere. I lived in books and in the wonderful stories my grandparents told me. The "stories" I told myself were my way of making up my own things I could believe in, trust, and love."

After the day's work was finished, the young Rosemary Catacalos heard stories from the mythology of her Greek ancestors. From her Hispanic mother, Catacalos learned the Spanish language, absorbing the rich folklore and traditions of that culture. Both her Greek and Hispanic ancestry have influenced her poetry, in particular the musicality of the Spanish language, which Catacalos often includes in her writings. Catacalos has won prizes for her poetry, has worked at promoting writing and literature in communities, and is a teacher. However, she tells us that she is "still learning, still going through new doors."

"The poems in this book are open doors inviting you into the world of making something good out of everything that touches you, even the bad stuff."

PAULA GUNN ALLEN (1939–   )

Taking a Visitor to See the Ruins

for Joe Bruchac

He's still telling about the time he came west
and was visiting me. I knew he
wanted to see some of the things

everybody sees when they're in the wilds of New Mexico.
5   So when we'd had our morning coffee
after he'd arrived, I said,

Would you like to go see some old Indian ruins?
His eyes brightened with excitement,
he was thinking, no doubt,

10   of places like the ones he'd known where he came from,
sacred caves filled with falseface masks,
ruins long abandoned, built secure

into the sacred lands; or of pueblos
once home to vanished people but peopled still
15   by their ghosts, connected still with the bone-old land.

Sure, he said. I'd like that a lot.
Come on, I said, and we got in my car,
drove a few blocks east, toward the towering peaks

of the Sandias. We stopped at a tall
20   high-security apartment building made of stone,
went up a walk past the pond and pressed the buzzer.

They answered and we went in,
past the empty pool room, past the empty party room,
up five flights in the elevator, down the abandoned hall.

25 Joe, I said when we'd gotten inside the chic apartment,
    I'd like you to meet the old Indian ruins
    I promised.

    My mother, Mrs. Francis, and my grandmother, Mrs. Gottlieb.
    His eyes grew large, and then he laughed
30 looking shocked at the two

    women he'd just met. Silent for a second, they laughed too.
    And he's still telling the tale of the old
    Indian ruins he visited in New Mexico,

    the two who still live pueblo style in high-security dwellings
35 way up there where the enemy can't reach them
    just like in the olden times.

What the Moon Said

The moon lives in all the alone places
all alone.
  "There are things
  I work out for myself," she says.
5   "You don't have to be depressed about them.
  These are my paces, and walking through them
        is my right.
  You don't need to care
    when I'm down.
10   "Or if I'm mad at myself, don't believe
      I'm mad at you.
  If I glare it is not your face I am staring at
     but my own.
  If I weep, it is not your tears that flow.

15   "And if I glow
  with the brush of twilight wings,
  if I rise round and warm
    above your bed,
  if I sail
20   through the iridescent°
      autumn spaces
  heavy with promise,
    with red and fruity light,
  and leave your breath
25   tangled in the tossing tops
  of trees as I arise,
  as I speed away into the far distance,
  disappearing as you gaze,
  turning silver, turning white,

---

20. iridescent (ir'i•des'ənt): showing the shifting colors of the rainbow.

30   it is not your glory I reflect.
        It is not your love
            that makes me pink,

                        copper,

                            gold.

35   It is mine."
      The moon moves along the sky by her own willing.
      It is her nature to shed some light, sometimes
      to be full and close, heavy with unborn thought
      on rising. It is her nature sometimes
40   to wander in some distant place, hidden, absent, gone.

MEET THE *Poet*

PAULA GUNN ALLEN

Paula Gunn Allen was a middle child, with two older sisters and two younger brothers. She is also a child of several cultures— Lebanese, Sioux, and Laguna Pueblo. Allen grew up in Cubero, New Mexico. Cubero is a village close to the Laguna and Acoma reservations. It was settled more than six hundred years ago.

In "Taking a Visitor to See the Ruins," Allen surprises her visitor and the reader by taking them to visit her mother and

grandmother, who live in a high-rise apartment building. Allen introduces the women as the "old Indian ruins," and everyone laughs. The poem is more than a joke, however. Allen implies that the two women living at the top of the apartment building are living in much the same manner as the ancient Pueblo Indians, perched high out of the reach of their enemies. In other ways, the building's abandoned and empty pool room, party room, and hallway are like today's Indian ruins—also forsaken and empty.

Her feeling of connection with her American Indian past is important to Allen and this connection has helped her develop independence and a sense of pride. "What the Moon Said" is a statement of this independent spirit.

LUCILLE CLIFTON

From the very beginning, Clifton knew that she did *not* want to be ordinary.

Certainly there is no one today who would describe Clifton as ordinary. Clifton is an African American woman who is also a poet—not an ordinary occupation. Even in her poetry, Clifton is different from other poets, with a style all her own.

Her poems are usually short and in free verse, with no punctuation. Reading one of Clifton's poems, you are guided by

the care she takes in her choice and grouping of words. In "my lost father," for example, her first line contains only four words but those words create an instant image. Clifton does not describe the lost father, she does not give details of his appearance or tell us what he says. She tells us to look at him and see him moving—and we do. The absence of commas, periods, and other punctuation in this, and Clifton's other poems, is made up for by the careful placement of each word and each line. We look at the poem on the page and know how it should sound.

Clifton has a gifted way with words—she does not use many words, but those she does employ in her poetry are stimulating and appeal to our emotions. In "why some people be mad at me sometimes," Clifton helps the reader remember all those times when being stubbornly oneself caused others to be angry. She is also alluding, or referring, to a larger and more universal situation—that of African Americans being asked to remember their past the way whites want it remembered. Clifton does all this in five lines and nineteen words.

Clifton uses many forms of repetition to make her point in her poems. In "move," Clifton writes of an actual historical event that involved a group that called itself Move. She repeats the words *move* and *away,* playing with their meanings so that in the end, *move away* becomes a command.

Clifton went to college very early, at sixteen years of age, and began to develop her own style as a poet in her late teens and early twenties, while she was working as an actor. Throughout her writing career, Clifton has remained constant in her belief that each person should be true to his or her own self and not accept other people's definitions. In all her writing she tries to write what is true—that is, what her heart or her emotions tell her is true. "I . . . take seriously the responsibility of not lying. . . . It's the truth as I see it, and that's what my responsibility is."

Clifton's gifts as an actor carry the audiences at her public readings right along with her. At these performances, Clifton chooses some poems that she wants to hear, but responds to each group with the poems she feels they want to hear. Clifton compares her experience at these readings to surfing on a wave. For Clifton, riding the emotional high that the audience gives her is both serious and fun.

Certainly Clifton's life and her work are not ordinary. She has taught herself to write poetry that speaks to everyone—simply, directly, and truthfully. This is the work of an extraordinary woman.

LUCILLE CLIFTON (1936–   )

my lost father

see where he moves
he leaves a wake of tears
see in the path of his going
the banners of regret
5   see just above him the cloud
of welcome   see him rise
see him enter the company
of husbands   fathers   sons

[the bodies broken on]

the bodies broken on
the Trail of Tears°
and the bodies melted
in Middle Passage°

5   are married to rock and
ocean by now
and the mountains crumbling on
white men
the waters pulling white men down

10   sing for red dust and black clay
good news about the earth

2. **Trail of Tears:** The forced westward march of the Cherokee population in 1838, during which thousands perished from hunger and hardship.
4. **Middle Passage:** The route of the slave trade across the Atlantic from West Africa to the West Indies or America.

move°

they had begun to whisper
among themselves   hesitant
to be branded neighbor to the wild
haired women the naked children
5   reclaiming a continent
away

move

he hesitated
then turned his smoky finger
10 toward africa toward the house
he might have lived in might have
owned or saved had he not turned
away

move

15 the helicopter rose at the command
higher at first then hesitating
then turning toward the center
of its own town only a neighborhood
away

20 move

she cried as the child stood
hesitant in the last clear sky
he would ever see the last
before the whirling blades the whirling smoke

move: refers to the bombing of the residence of an African American back-to-nature group
calling itself Move. Members wore dreadlocks and took the surname Africa. The bombing was
ordered by Philadelphia's first African American mayor after complaints by the neighbors. Eleven
people, including some children, were killed and sixty-one homes were destroyed.

25 and sharp debris carried all clarity
away

move

if you live in a mind
that would destroy itself
30 to comfort itself
if you would stand fire
rather than difference
do not hesitate
move
35 away

why some people be mad at me sometimes

they ask me to remember
but they want me to remember
their memories
and i keep on remembering
5   mine.

4 daughters

i am the sieve° she strains from
little by little
everyday.

i am the rind°
5   she is discarding.

i am the riddle
she is trying to answer.

something is moving
in the water.
10 she is the hook.
i am the line.

1. **sieve** (sĭv): a container with holes in the bottom, used for straining. Dirt and grit can be washed from vegetables in a sieve.
4. **rind:** the skin of an apple, orange, banana, or other fruit. Often the rind is discarded.

in the inner city

In the inner city
or
like we call it
home
5   we think a lot about uptown
and the silent nights
and the houses straight as
dead men
and the pastel lights
10 and we hang on to our no place
happy to be alive
and in the inner city
or like we call it
home

Ways to Tell a Story

Many early poems were composed as a way of telling about events that were important to people. Some of these early poems were songs, passed down for generations.

As these poems developed, they took on different characteristics. A **narrative** poem tells a long story, like the mysterious story told in "Flannan Isle," which appears in this section. A shorter, songlike poem that tells a story is a **ballad**. These are told or sung in simple language with repeated lines or refrains that make them easy to remember. There are several ballads in this section—all telling a tragic or adventurous story.

The **spiritual** and the **blues song** also tell a short, emotionally laden story. Spirituals tell the story of African Americans and slavery. Some spirituals carried hidden messages and were guides to freedom for enslaved people. The blues tell many kinds of stories—about men and locomotives, natural disasters, superstitions—but may be best known for their love stories.

The framework for an extremely short story is the **haiku,** a form that developed in Japan. The poet who writes the haiku wants you, the reader, to supply details from common experiences that set the scene and the mood of the story.

Each of these poetic forms has its own effect. The often slow-moving and rhythmic refrains of blues songs and spirituals build gradually to an emotional effect. The haiku's quick change from image to image leads to a moment of clear understanding.

Cultural background helps determine the way a poet chooses to write. The story-telling traditions of the English and Spanish cultures gave rise to early folk ballads. Similarly, Zen Buddhism, with its emphasis on encouraging students to gain insights for themselves, influenced the haiku.

A poet's desire to tell a story has given us some of our most enduring poetry and songs, a few of which you will read in this chapter.

WILFRID WILSON GIBSON
(1878–1962)

Flannan Isle

"Though three men dwell on Flannan Isle
To keep the lamp alight,
As we steered under the lee,° we caught
No glimmer through the night!"

5   A passing ship at dawn had brought
The news; and quickly we set sail,
To find out what strange thing might ail°
The keepers of the deep-sea light.
The winter day broke blue and bright,
10   With glancing sun and glancing spray,
While o'er the swell our boat made way,
As gallant as a gull in flight.

But as we neared the lonely Isle,
And looked up at the naked height,
15   And saw the lighthouse towering white,
With blinded lantern that all night
Had never shot a spark
Of comfort through the dark,
So ghostly in the cold sunlight
20   It seemed that we were struck the while
With wonder all too dread for words.

And as into the tiny creek
We stole beneath the hanging crag,
We saw three queer, black, ugly birds—

3. **lee:** sheltered side of the island.
7. **ail:** the cause of distress.

25 Too big by far in my belief

 For guillemot or shag°—

 Like seamen sitting bolt upright

 Upon a half-tide reef;

 But as we neared, they plunged from sight

30 Without a sound or spurt of white.

 And still too mazed° to speak,

 We landed, and made fast the boat,

 And climbed the track in single file—

 Each wishing he were safe afloat

35 On any sea, however far,

 So be it far from Flannan Isle:

 And still we seemed to climb and climb,

 As though we'd lost all count of time,

 And so must climb forevermore.

40 Yet all too soon we reached the door—

 The black, sun-blistered lighthouse door,

 That gaped for us ajar.

 As on the threshold for a spell

 We paused, we seemed to breathe the smell

45 Of limewash and of tar,

 Familiar as our daily breath,

 As though 'twere some strange scent of death:

 And so, yet wondering, side by side

 We stood a moment, still tongue-tied:

50 And each with black foreboding eyed

 The door, ere we should fling it wide

 To leave the sunlight for the gloom:

 Till, plucking courage up, at last

---

26. guillemot (gil'ə•mät') **or shag:** species of seabird.
31. mazed: dazed or bewildered.

Hard on each other's heels we passed
55 Into the living room.

Yet as we crowded through the door,
We only saw a table, spread
For dinner, meat and cheese and bread;
But all untouched; and no one there;
60 As though when they sat down to eat,
Ere they could even taste,
Alarm had come; and they in haste
Had risen and left the bread and meat:
For at the table-head a chair
65 Lay tumbled on the floor.
We listened; but we only heard
The feeble chirping of a bird
That starved upon its perch:
And, listening still, without a word
70 We set about our hopeless search.

We hunted high, we hunted low;
And soon ransacked the empty house;
Then o'er the island, to and fro,
We ranged, to listen and to look
75 In every cranny, cleft, or nook
That might have hid a bird or mouse.
But though we searched from shore to shore,
We found no sign in any place:
And soon again stood face to face
80 Before the gaping door:
And stole into the room once more
As frightened children steal.

Ay: though we hunted high and low,
And hunted everywhere,

85   Of the three men's fate we found no trace
      Of any kind in any place,
      But a door ajar, and an untouched meal,
      And an overtoppled chair.

      And so we listened in the gloom
90   Of that forsaken living room—
      A chill clutch on our breath—
      We thought how ill-chance came to all
      Who kept the Flannan Light;
      And how the rock had been the death
95   Of many a likely lad;
      How six had come to a sudden end,
      And three had gone stark mad:

      And one whom we'd all known as friend
      Had leapt from the lantern one still night,
100   And fallen dead by the lighthouse wall:
      And long we thought
      On the three we sought,
      And of what might yet befall.

      Like curs a glance has brought to heel,
105   We listened, flinching there:
      And looked, and looked, on the untouched meal
      And the overtoppled chair.

      We seemed to stand for an endless while,
      Though still no word was said,
110   Three men alive on Flannan Isle,
      Who thought on three men dead.

MEET THE *Poet*

WILFRID WILSON GIBSON

Almost everyone loves a mystery, and the mysterious happening on which Wilfrid Wilson Gibson based "Flannan Isle" was a bizarre, real-life incident. On December 26, 1900, the Flannan Lighthouse was found deserted and the lighthouse beam dark. The three lighthouse keepers had disappeared, leaving no trace behind. This incident at the lonely lighthouse in the Outer Hebrides off the coast of Scotland was the inspiration for Gibson's poem.

How did Gibson come to write this long, mysterious story as a poem? Gibson wanted to write about real life; about the experiences and occupations of ordinary people, such as the three

men who manned the lighthouse on Flannan Isle. Not all poets who were writing at this time felt this way; many felt that poetry should be about historical or mythological happenings written in high-flown, complicated language.

As well as writing about ordinary people, Gibson wanted to bring together stage drama and verse. Imagine how pleased and excited Gibson would have been to be in the audience for the opening in 1980 of an opera called *The Lighthouse,* which was based on the Flannan Isle lighthouse mystery. Gibson would have been even more excited at the very odd thing that happened on the day *The Lighthouse* opened. The real Flannan Isle's light, which was now automatic, went out, and a helicopter had to take a crew out to restart it.

GARRETT HONGO (1951–)

Eruption: Pu'u O'o

We woke near midnight,
flicking on the coat closet's bulb,
the rainforest chilled with mist,
a yellow swirl of gas
5   in the spill of light outside.
Stars paling, tucked high
in the sky's blue jade,
we saw, through the back windows
and tops of *ohi'a*° trees,
10   silhouettes and red showers
as if from Blake's fires,°
magenta and billows of black volleying.
Then, a burbling underground,
like rice steaming in the pot,
15   shook through chandeliers of fern
and the A-frame's tambourine floor,
stirring the cats and chickens
from the crawl-space and their furled sleep.
The fountain rose to 900 feet that night,
20   without us near it, smoking white,
spitting from the cone 6 miles away,
a geyser of flame, pyramids and gyres° of ash.
Novices,° we dressed and drove out,
first to the crater rim, Uwekahuna
25   a canyon and sea of ash and moonstone,

9. ohi'a: Hawaiian word for myrtle tree.
11. Blake's fires: English poet William Blake (1757–1827) described the fires of Hell.
22. gyres (jīrz): a motion that is circular and spiraling.
23. novices: people who are new to an event or happening.

the hardened, grey back of Leviathan°
steaming and venting,° dormant under cloud-cover.
And then next down Volcano Road past the villages
to Hirano Store on Kilauea's long plateau.

30   There, over canefield and the hardened lava land,
all we saw was in each other's eyes—
the mind's fear and the heart's delight,
running us this way and that.

26. Leviathan (lə•vīˈə•thən): a huge sea creature, perhaps a whale, that is mentioned in
the Bible.
27. venting: letting gas or steam escape through a small opening.

The Legend

In Chicago, it is snowing softly
and a man has just done his wash for the week.
He steps into the twilight of early evening,
carrying a wrinkled shopping bag
5   full of neatly folded clothes,
and, for a moment, enjoys
the feel of warm laundry and crinkled paper,
flannellike against his gloveless hands.
There's a Rembrandt glow on his face,
10   a triangle of orange in the hollow of his cheek
as a last flash of sunset
blazes the storefronts and lit windows of the street.

He is Asian, Thai or Vietnamese,
and very skinny, dressed as one of the poor
15   in rumpled suit pants and a plaid mackinaw,°
dingy and too large.
He negotiates the slick of ice
on the sidewalk by his car,
opens the Fairlane's back door,
20   leans to place the laundry in,
and turns, for an instant,
toward the flurry of footsteps
and cries of pedestrians
as a boy—that's all he was—
25   backs from the corner package store
shooting a pistol, firing it,
once, at the dumbfounded man
who falls forward,
grabbing at his chest.

15. mackinaw: garment made from heavy woolen cloth.

30   A few sounds escape from his mouth,
         a babbling no one understands
         as people surround him
         bewildered at his speech.
         The noises he makes are nothing to them.

35   The boy has gone, lost
         in the light array of foot traffic
         dappling the snow with fresh prints.

         Tonight, I read about Descartes'°
         grand courage to doubt everything
40   except his own miraculous existence
         and I feel so distinct
         from the wounded man lying on the concrete
         I am ashamed.

         Let the night sky cover him as he dies.
45   Let the weaver girl° cross the bridge of heaven°
         and take up his cold hands.

38. Descartes (dā•kärt'): French philosopher and mathematician, 1596–1650.
45. weaver girl: gave up being with her lover to weave the beauty that clothes the universe.
    bridge of heaven: where the weaver girl and her lover meet once a year.

MEET THE *Poet*

GARRETT HONGO

Garrett Hongo brought his wife and baby boy back to see the place where he was born, the Hawaiian town of Volcano. In the middle of the night, they were shaken awake—the ground was rocking and swaying, there were underground rumblings and the landscape was lit with an eerie red glow. The volcano Kilauea was erupting. Hongo went back to bed—volcanic eruptions were nothing new to him—but his wife had never seen a volcano erupt and was terrified. Hongo wrote "Eruption: Pu'u O'o" in response to his wife's fear. He also wanted to celebrate the magnificence of the volcano.

The writing of Hongo's second poem in this collection, "The Legend," changed the poet's life. He decided to give up his academic career and instead write a book of poems. "The Legend" is linked to Hongo's past through the Asian legend about the River of Heaven, or Milky Way. In the story, the River of Heaven separates two lovers: a goatherd and the weaver girl. The weaver girl has the job of weaving together the beauty that clothes the universe. Because her task is so difficult, the weaver girl must give up being with her lover, the goatherd boy. However, once a year the universe takes pity on her and allows the two lovers to be united when an accidental action makes a bridge across the River of Heaven. The anonymous Asian man, slain on the streets of Chicago, becomes that bridge, and is himself taken across to heaven by the weaver girl.

ANONYMOUS

The Ballad of Gregorio Cortez

1

In the county of El Carmen,
The misfortune has occurred;
The Major Sheriff died,
Leaving Román badly wounded.

2

5   In the county of El Carmen,
The misfortune occurred;
The Major Sheriff died;
It is not known who killed him.

3

He went out toward Laredo,°
10   Without showing any fear,
"Follow me, you cowardly rangers,
I am Gregorio Cortez."

4

Then said Gregorio Cortez,
And his soul was all aflame,
15   "I don't regret that I killed him;
A man must defend himself."

5

Then said Gregorio Cortez,
With his pistol in his hand,
"Don't run, you cowardly rangers,
20   From a real Mexican."

9. Laredo (lah•reh'doh): city and port of entry in South Texas.

146   Music, Pictures, and Stories

6

It must have been about eight o'clock,
About three hours afterward,
They found out that the wrongdoer
Had been Gregorio Cortez.

7

25 The Americans were riding
Through the air as if they flew;
Because they wanted to get
Two thousand dollars they were offered.

8

Then the Americans said,
30 "If we find him, what shall we do?
If we fight him man to man
Very few of us will return."

9

The Americans were riding,
They were following the trail;
35 Because trying to overtake Cortez
Was like overtaking a star.

10

Then said Gregorio Cortez,
"What is the use of your scheming?
You cannot catch me,
40 Even with those bloodhounds."

11

Gregorio says to Juan,
"You will see it very soon;
Go tell the rangers
To come and arrest me."

12

45   Over by El Encinal°
They succeeded in surrounding him;
Quite a few more than three hundred,
But there he jumped their corral.

13

Gregorio Cortez went out,
50   He went out toward Laredo,
They decided not to follow
Because they were afraid of him.

14

All the rangers were coming,
They were looking for Cortez;
55   They asked of many people,
"Where is the ranch of El Ciprés?"°

15

When the rangers arrived,
Gregorio gave himself up,
"You will take me if I'm willing,
60   But not any other way."

16

Now they have killed Cortez,
Now matters are at an end;
His poor family
Are suffering in their hearts.

17

65   Now with this I say farewell,
With the leaves of the cypress,
This is the end of the ballad
Of Don Gregorio Cortez.

45. El Encinal (ehl ehn•see•nahl'): literally "The Woods"; the name of a village in South
Texas.
56. El Ciprés (ehl see•prehs'): literally "The Cypress"; the name of a ranch in South Texas.

ANONYMOUS

The Cowboy's Lament

As I walked out in the streets of Laredo,
As I walked out in Laredo one day,
I spied a poor cowboy wrapped up in white linen
Wrapped up in white linen as cold as the clay.

5 "Oh beat the drum slowly and play the fife lowly,
Play the dead march as you carry me along;
Take me to the green valley, there lay the sod o'er me,
For I'm a young cowboy and I know I've done wrong.

"I see by your outfit that you are a cowboy"—
10 These words he did say as I boldly stepped by.
"Come sit down beside me and hear my sad story;
I am shot in the breast and I know I must die.

"Let sixteen gamblers come handle my coffin,
Let sixteen cowboys come sing me a song.
15 Take me to the graveyard and lay the sod o'er me,
For I'm a poor cowboy and I know I've done wrong.

"My friends and relations they live in the Nation,°
They know not where their boy has gone.
He first came to Texas and hired to a ranchman
20 Oh, I'm a young cowboy and I know I've done wrong.

"It was once in the saddle I used to go dashing,
It was once in the saddle I used to go gay;
First to the dramhouse° and then to the cardhouse;
Got shot in the breast and I am dying today.

17. **Nation:** United States. The ballad is set before 1845, when Texas became part of the
    United States.
23. **dramhouse:** saloon.

25   "Get six jolly cowboys to carry my coffin;
       Get six pretty maidens to bear up my pall.
       Put bunches of roses all over my coffin,
       Put roses to deaden the sods as they fall.

       "Then swing your rope slowly and rattle your spurs lowly,
30   And give a wild whoop as you carry me along;
       And in the grave throw me and roll the sod o'er me
       For I'm a young cowboy and I know I've done wrong.

       "Oh, bury beside me my knife and six-shooter,
       My spurs on my heel, my rifle by my side,
35   And over my coffin put a bottle of brandy.
       That the cowboys may drink as they carry me along.

       "Go bring me a cup, a cup of cold water,
       To cool my parched lips," the cowboy then said;
       Before I returned his soul had departed,
40   And gone to the roundup—the cowboy was dead.

       We beat the drum slowly and played the fife lowly,
       And bitterly wept as we bore him along;
       For we all loved our comrade, so brave, young, and handsome,
       We all loved our comrade although he'd done wrong.

MEET THE *Poet*

THE BALLADEER

Many popular songwriters, like Bob Dylan and Willie Nelson, write ballads. Just as in the older ballads, their songs tell a story of a hero or of heroic events in poetic form. A big difference, of course, is that modern songwriters are famous, while the names of the composers of traditional ballads will never be known.

Ballads have always been an important form of literature in both England and Spain. As the Americas were colonized, ballads found a natural home, telling the stories of mountain and plain, of work and play, of the railroad worker and the lonesome cowboy. Both ballads here include details we have come to associate with the cowboy—a six-shooter, spurs, horses, rope, and the roundup.

Ballads can express strong emotions. "The Ballad of Gregorio Cortez" is about someone larger than life, whose unjust death at the hands of the rangers causes his family to suffer. "The Cowboy's Lament" is about the death of someone too young to die.

Another favorite theme of the folk ballad is tragic love, sometimes between two people of different families or cultures, very much like Shakespeare's story of Romeo and Juliet. Whatever the theme, the strong, simple language and the genuine emotion of the ballad make it a favorite of people of any time, including ours.

E. E. CUMMINGS (1894–1962)

All in green went my love riding

All in green went my love riding
on a great horse of gold
into the silver dawn.

four lean hounds crouched low and smiling
5   the merry deer ran before.

Fleeter be they than dappled° dreams
the swift sweet deer
the red rare° deer

Four red roebuck° at a white water
10   the cruel bugle sang before.

Horn at hip went my love riding
riding the echo down
into the silver dawn.

four lean hounds crouched low and smiling
15   the level meadows ran before.

Softer be they than slippered sleep
the lean lithe deer
the fleet flown deer.

Four fleet does at a gold valley
20   the famished arrow sang before

Bow at belt went my love riding
riding the mountain down
into the silver dawn.

6. **dappled:** speckled.
8. **rare:** very fine.
9. **roebuck:** male roe deer, a type of small, swift deer.

four lean hounds crouched low and smiling
25 the sheer peaks ran before.

Paler be they than daunting° death
the sleek slim deer
the tall tense deer.

Four tall stags at a green mountain
30 the lucky hunter sang before.

All in green went my love riding
on a great horse of gold
into the silver dawn.

four lean hounds crouched low and smiling
35 my heart fell dead before.

26. daunting: frightening.

MEET THE *Poet*

E. E. CUMMINGS

Can you imagine how good you would be at any sport if you practiced every day for fourteen years? Or how well you would learn a language? Or how much you would know about any subject under the sun?

That's exactly how E. E. Cummings became a poet. He wrote a poem every day for fourteen years, between the ages of eight and twenty-two. By the time Cummings went to college, he was skilled at writing traditional poetry but soon began to write poetry that ignored capital letters and standard punctuation.

In 1917, the First World War was being fought in Europe, though America was not yet involved. Like Ernest Hemingway, another young man who was to become famous as a writer, Cummings volunteered for ambulance service. Cummings had some war tales to tell— he was suspected of espionage and held for months by the French because of the exasperating and mysterious comments he made in the letters he wrote home.

Famous for his love poems, Cummings also wrote poems with a political message. He was very suspicious of groups, governments, or anything that hinted of group thinking. Instead, he promoted the individual in his highly original style that seems as fresh today as it did back then.

ROY HELTON (1886–1977?)

Old Christmas

"Where are you coming from, Lomey Carter,
    So airly° over the snow?
And what's them pretties° you got in your hand,
    And where you aiming to go?

5   "Step in, honey! Old Christmas° morning
    I ain't got nothing much;
Maybe a bite of sweetness and corn bread,
    A little ham meat and such.

"But come in, honey! Sally Anne Barton's
10   Hungering after your face.
Wait till I light my candle up:
    Set down! There's your old place.

"Now where you been so airly this morning?"
    "Graveyard, Sally Anne.
15   *Up by the trace° in the salt-lick° meadows*
    Where Taulbe kilt my man."

"Taulbe ain't to home this morning. . . .
    I can't scratch up a light:
Dampness gets on the heads of the matches;
20   But I'll blow up the embers bright."

---

2. airly: early.
3. pretties: probably branches of elder bushes, which are supposed to bloom to honor Christ's birth in December.
5. Old Christmas: January 6th, the twelfth day of Christmas, is also know as Epiphany, Little Christmas, and Old Christmas. According to tradition, it was on this date that the Magi visited the infant Jesus. In some places, the birth of Jesus is celebrated on this day, and gifts are exchanged.
15. trace: path
    salt-lick: a place where there is mineral salt which animals lick; therefore, good hunting ground.

"Needn't trouble. I won't be stopping:
  Going a long ways still."
"You didn't see nothing, Lomey Carter,
  Up on the graveyard hill?"

25 *"What should I see there, Sally Anne Barton?"*
    "Well, sperits do walk last night."
"There were an elder bush° a-blooming
  While the moon still give some light."

"Yes, elder bushes, they bloom, Old Christmas,
30   And critters kneel down in their straw.
Anything else up in the graveyard?"

    "One thing more I saw:
I saw my man with his head all bleeding
  Where Taulbe's shot went through."

35 "What did he say?"
                    "He stooped and kissed me."
    "What did he say to you?"

"Said, Lord Jesus forguv your Taulbe;
  But he told me another word;
40 *He said it soft when he stooped and kissed me.*
  That were the last I heard."

"Taulbe ain't to home this morning."
    "I know that, Sally Anne,
For I kilt him coming down through the meadow
45   *Where Taulbe kilt my man.*

"I met him upon the meadow trace
  When the moon were fainting fast,
And I had my dead man's rifle gun

---

27. elder bush: a shrub which usually blooms in the summer.

And kilt him as he came past."

50   "But I heard two shots."

                 "'Twas his was second:
    He shot me 'fore he died:
    You'll find us at daybreak, Sally Anne Barton:
    I'm laying there dead at his side."

MEET THE *Poet*

ROY HELTON

Born over one hundred years ago in 1886, it took Roy Helton awhile to discover his direction in life. After high school, Helton attended the University of Pennsylvania, where he studied art. Unfortunately, Helton discovered that he was colorblind. Then he tried being an inventor but again, without success. Eventually Helton became a schoolmaster in Pennsylvania.

Helton's ancestors lived in the Appalachian hill country and he developed an interest in the people who lived there, spending time in the mountains of South Carolina and Kentucky. As a result, the language of the mountain people found its way into many of his poems and stories, as it does in "Old Christmas." Though he tried to use only the most common words from the vocabulary of these people, the two women talking in this ballad sometimes use words that may seem unusual to today's readers.

And so it was that Roy Helton, the failed inventor and colorblind art student, became a successful writer. He published novels, stories, and poems, many of them influenced by the language and culture of the mountain people he grew to know and love.

BESSIE SMITH (1894–1937)

Backwater Blues

When it rains five days and the skies turn dark as night,
When it rains five days and the skies turn dark as night,
Then trouble's takin' place in the lowlands at night.

I woke up this mornin', can't even get out of my door
5   I woke up this mornin', can't even get out of my door
That's enough trouble to make a poor girl wonder where
        she want to go.

Then they rowed a little boat about five miles 'cross the farm.
Then they rowed a little boat about five miles 'cross the farm.
I packed all my clothes, throwed them in and they rowed me
        along.

10   When it thunders and lightnin', and the wind begins to blow,
When it thunders and lightnin', and the wind begins to blow,
There's thousands of people ain't got no place to go.

Then I went and stood upon some high old lonesome hill.
Then I went and stood upon some high old lonesome hill.
15   Then I looked down on the house where I used to live.

Backwater blues done caused me to pack my things and go.
Backwater blues done caused me to pack my things and go.
'Cause my house fell down and I can't live there no more.

(Moan) . . . . I can't move no more,
20   (Moan) . . . . I can't move no more,
There ain't no place for a poor old girl to go.

MEET THE *Poet*

BESSIE SMITH

Bessie Smith's exact birth date is not known but it is thought to have been around 1894. What is known exactly, however, is that in 1923 she became a singing sensation. By some reports, her first recording, "Down Hearted Blues," sold over two million copies the first year alone. Even today, that would make her a top selling star. By the time she died of injuries suffered in a car accident in 1937, she had made one hundred sixty recordings.

Though her career had begun to decline by the time of her death, Bessie Smith and her music are still important. During the folk music revival that began in the 1960s, she was recognized as someone who had helped to give shape to that type of singing known as the blues.

Blues singing seems to have grown out of the work songs of the early days of slavery in the American South. The way lines are repeated in blues songs is very like the call-and-response patterns of certain African songs. The repeating of lines is also found in the music of the early Protestant churches in the United States, so church music seems to have had some influence as well.

Today, many entertainers and fans of the blues know the music of Bessie Smith. With their themes of love and personal suffering, blues songs such as Bessie sang have had a profound influence on popular music in America and around the world.

ANONYMOUS

No More Auction Block

No more auction block for me,
No more, no more,
No more auction block for me,
Many thousand gone.

5   No more peck of corn° for me,
No more, no more,
No more peck of corn for me,
Many thousand gone.

No more pint of salt for me,
10   No more, no more,
No more pint of salt for me
Many thousand gone.

No more driver's lash for me,
No more, no more,
15   No more driver's lash for me,
Many thousand gone.

5. peck of corn: A reference to the limited rations—corn, and in the next stanza, salt—
granted the slave.

MEET THE *Poet*

SPIRITUALS

Spirituals, like ballads and blues songs, are a form of American folk poetry. Folk literature has no known authors and is simply spoken or sung. It is learned and added to for many years before it is written down. The spirituals of the enslaved people in the American South were produced in just this way. Their origin stretches back to the beginnings of slavery in the early colonies, but the songs were not written down and published until the 1800s.

Spirituals are more than just religious songs. By all accounts, they were sung on all occasions, at work or at play, as well as at church. One reason for this may be the wonderfully expressive quality of the language. The songs speak of "going home" to a better world, of a release from bondage, and of a just God who understands suffering.

The language of spirituals frequently has more than one meaning, adding complexity and interest. For example, the "Pharaoh" of Biblical times is linked to slave-holders and overseers, just as "Egypt" can be identified with the American South. The importance of Moses, who led the Israelites to freedom in "the Promised Land," is then easily understood.

The exact method by which a song or a poem is produced by a group rather than by an individual is not easily understood. Luckily, we do not have to understand the process in order to feel the impact of these beautiful and emotionally powerful songs.

Six Haiku

translated by **Harry Behn**

1   It is nice to read
news that our spring rain also
      visited your town.

                      —Onitsura

2   How cool cut hay smells
when carried through the farm gate
      as the sun comes up!

                      —Boncho

3   After the bells hummed
and were silent, flowers chimed
      a peal of fragrance.

                      —Basho

4   Broken and broken
again on the sea, the moon
      so easily mends.

                      —Chosu

5   Tonight in this town
where I was born, my only
      friends are the crickets.

                      —Anon.

6   I must go begging
for water . . . morning glories
        have captured my well.

               —Chiyo

MEET THE *Poet*

HAIKU

The techniques of writing haiku, one of Japan's most famous poetic forms, have often been compared to the techniques of painting or making movies. Haiku present pictures of the world around us, moving quickly from one image to the next. The reader connects the images based on his or her own experiences.

The rules for writing haiku are fairly strict. The most common is the "seventeen syllable" rule: the poem must consist of three lines—five syllables in the first line, seven syllables in the second, and five syllables in the last line. You can ignore the seventeen syllable rule but your haiku must have three lines. Another rule is that the poem must contain a word or image suggesting a season of the year. Furthermore, the haiku must not explain itself. The images of the poem must suggest their meaning to the reader with the end result being a flash of understanding—a moment when all the parts of the poem come together at once and "enlighten" the reader.

As challenging as these small poems are to write, they provide an exciting and imaginative way to provide the framework for a very brief story. You might like to try your hand at haiku. Use the word *haiku* as a keyword on any computer search engine. You will find hundreds of links to help you get started.

JIMMY SANTIAGO BACA

Does poetry matter? At one time in his life, Jimmy Santiago Baca might have answered that question with a loud "No!" "You couldn't do *anything* with a book," he said in an interview. "You couldn't fix a '57 Chevy with a book." Yet books and writing—and especially poetry—turned Baca's life around.

After his parents abandoned him at the age of two, Baca lived with relatives, was sent to an orphanage, and wound up living on the streets by the time he was ten. Drifting from state to state and in and out of trouble, he landed in prison on drug charges at the

age of twenty-one. Baca's story might have ended there, in the cell of a maximum-security prison in Arizona. But it did not. He had taught himself to read and write, and he was determined to have his voice heard.

In poetry, Baca found a way to tell his story. The poems are about what he knows firsthand—prison life, the people and places of the American Southwest, and his own struggle with anger and rage. Jimmy Santiago Baca is completely present in his poems. You do not have to read his biography to know that he was in prison; he tells you so in "It Started." You feel that he has lived in Santa Fe, New Mexico, when you read "Bells." You can hear his heritage in his mixed use of Spanish and English and in the details of his poems.

Some people would classify Baca as a "prison writer," and some would label him as a Chicano or Latino or Mexican American poet. He has a lot to say about prison, of course, and yes, his

Hispanic and Indian heritage is important in his poetry. But Jimmy Santiago Baca is able to take specific, personal experiences and observations and give them universal meanings.

When you read these poems, you will see that they are in free verse. Free verse is poetry without a regular meter or a rhyme scheme. Poets writing in free verse try to capture the natural rhythms of ordinary speech. It can be difficult to find the usual poetic elements in poems like these. However, read "Bells," out loud, and you can hear the growing, tumbling pile of verbs that help to create the poem's rhythm. In "Day's Blood," you can see how the image of the dogs changes in only eighteen short lines. In all the poems, you can see how a poem that starts out telling a personal story takes off and becomes something else—something *more*—by its end.

In Baca's poems, you can hear the emotional pain and struggle of his life, but you will also find an exuberant celebration of the human spirit. For Jimmy Santiago Baca, the most powerful tool human beings have is language, and he knows that poetry matters—after all, poetry saved his life.

JIMMY SANTIAGO BACA
(1952–   )

It Started

A little state-funded barrack
in the desert, in a prison. A poetry workshop,
an epicenter of originality, companionship,
pain and openness,

5
      For some,
the first time in their life writing,
for others the first time saying openly what they felt,
the first time finding something in themselves,
worthwhile, ugly and beautiful.

10
     I think of you and me. Last night I was
thinking of you. I am your friend. I don't want you
to think otherwise.

     I was thinking, when we first wrote to each other.
     I remember instances, of tremendous joy
15
     when receiving your letters,
     what cells I was in,
     what emotional state, under
     what circumstances.
     Your letters always fell like meteorites
20
     into my lap.
     You were my first friendship
     engendered in this state, perhaps,
     all my past life.

I showed you my first poem ever written,

"They Only Came to See the Zoo"

But you didn't treat me like a wild ape,
or an elephant. You treated me like Jimmy.
And who was Jimmy?
A mass of molten fury in this furnace of steel,
30 and yet, my thoughts became ladles, sifting carefully
through my life, the pain and endurance,
to the essence of my being.
I gently, into the long night, unmolding
my shielded heart, the fierce figures
35 of war and loss, I remolding them,
my despair and anger into a cry and song.
I took the path alone, nuded myself to my own caged animals,
and learned their tongues and their spirits,
and roamed the desert, went to my place of birth. . . .
40 Now tonight, I am a burning bush,
my bones a grill of fire,
I burn these words in praise,
of our meeting, our friendship.

from Poem VI

Cruising back from 7–11
esta mañana°
in my '56 Chevy truckita,
beat up and rankled°
5   farm truck,
clanking between rows
of new shiny cars—

        "Hey fella! Trees need pruning
        and the grass needs trimming!"
10   A man yelled down to me
from his 3rd-story balcony.

        "Sorry, I'm not the gardener,"
        I yelled up to him.

Funny how in the Valley
15   an old truck symbolizes prestige°
and in the Heights, poverty.

Worth is determined in the Valley
by age and durability,°
and in the Heights, by newness
20   and impression.

In the Valley,
the atmosphere is soft and worn,
things are shared and passed down.
In the Heights,

---

2. **esta mañana** (e'stä män•yä'nä): today.
4. **rankled** (raŋ'kəld): caused resentment and anger.
15. **prestige** (pres•tēzh'): success.
18. **durability** (door'ə•bil'ə•tē): ability to last despite hard use or advanced age.

25 the air is blistered with the glaze
 of new cars and new homes.

 How many days of my life
 I have spent fixing up
 rusty broken things,
30 charging up old batteries,
 wiring pieces of odds and ends together!
 Ah, those lovely bricks
 and sticks I found in the fields
 and took home with me
35 to make flower boxes!
 The old cars I've worked on
 endlessly giving them tune-ups,
 changing tires, tracing
 electrical shorts,
40 cursing when I've been stranded
 between Laguna pueblo° and Burque.°
 It's the process of making-do,
 of the life I've lived between
 breakdowns and break-ups, that has made life
45 worth living.

 I could not bear a life
 with everything perfect.

---

41. Laguna pueblo (lä'gōō•nä pweb'lō): six villages located about 40 miles west of **Burque** (bʉr'kē): shortened version of Albuquerque, town in New Mexico.

Day's Blood

I toss yesterday's tortillas
to pack dogs at my door—
with bared fangs and smoldering
matted scruff-fur hackles,°
5   they grunt-scarf then slouch away.
Snouts in weeds for more chance scraps,
in mournful whines and whimpers, heel-nipping,
with floppy, sagging, lopsided shuffle,
they cross fields towards the Oñate° Feedmill,
10   where they gnaw hooves and snarl
over gutted intestines
at the back door of the slaughterhouse.
At night they sleep in the Rio Grande bosque,°
and walking there myself at night,
15   in the moonlight,
I've seen their eyes glint in the brush,
bloody obsidian° knife blades
dripping with the day's blood.

   4. hackles (hak'əlz): fur on back of dog's neck and back.
   9. Oñate (ō•nyäh'tā)
  13. bosque (bôs'kā'): a small grove of trees.
  17. obsidian (əb•sid'ē•ən): black glass that is formed in a volcano.

Bells

Bells. The word gongs my skull . . .
Mama carried me out, just born,
swaddled in hospital blanket,
from St. Vincent's in Santa Fe.
5   Into the evening, still drowsed
with uterine° darkness,
my fingertips purple with new life,
cathedral bells splashed
into my blood, plunging iron hulls
10 into my pulse waves. Cathedral steeples,
amplified brooding, sonorous° bells,
through narrow cobbled streets, bricked patios,
rose trellis'd° windows,
red-tiled Spanish rooftops, bells
15 beat my name, "Santiago! Santiago!"
Burning my name in black-frosted streets,
bell sounds curved and gonged deep,
ungiving, full-bellowed beats of iron on iron,
shuddering pavement Mama walked,
20 quivering thick stainless panes, creaking
plaza shop doors, beating its gruff thuds
down alleys and dirt
passageways, past men waiting in doorways
of strange houses. Mama carried me past
25 peacocks and chickens, past the miraculous
stairwell winding into the choirloft, touted
in tourist brochures, *"Not one nail was used*

---

6. uterine (yo͞ot'ə•rin): of the womb, the organ in which a fetus grows into a baby.
11. sonorous (sə•nôr'əs): having a sound.
13. trellis'd (trel'ist): trellised, made up of strips of wood fastened together to form an open pattern.

to build this, it clings tenaciously°
together by pure prayer power, a spiraling
30   *pinnacle° of faith . . ."*And years later,
when I would do something wrong,
in kind reprimand Mama would say,
"You were born of bells, more than my womb,
they speak to you in dreams.
35   *Ay, Mejito,°*
you are such a dreamer!"

28. tenaciously (tə•nā'shəs•lē): strongly, firmly.
29. pinnacle (pin'ə•kəl): the highest part.
35. Mejito (mē•hē'tō): version of *mi hijito,* my little son.

Glossary of Literary Terms

For a poem that contains an example of a term, turn to the page(s) in this book indicated on a separate line at the end of the entries. For example, "The Cowboy's Lament," page 149, is a ballad.

On another line are cross-references to entries in this glossary that provide closely related terms. For instance, at the end of *Analogy* is a cross-reference to *Metaphor* and *Simile*.

ALLITERATION The repetition of the same or very similar consonant sounds in words that are close together. Though alliteration usually occurs at the beginning of words, it can also occur within or at the end of words. Among other things, alliteration can help establish a mood, emphasize words, and serve as a memory aid. In the following example the **s** sound is repeated at the beginning of the words *silken* and *sad* and within the words *uncertain* and *rustling*:

> And the **s**ilken **s**ad un**c**ertain ru**s**tling of each purple curtain
> —Edgar Allan Poe,
> from "The Raven"

See "Hector the Collector," page 4, line 5.
See "Latest Latin Dance Craze," page 22, line 17.

ALLUSION A reference to a statement, a person, a place, or an event from literature, history, religion, mythology, politics, sports, or science. Allusions enrich the reading experience. Writers expect readers to recognize an allusion and to think, almost at the same time, about the literary work and the person, place, or event that it refers to. The following lines, describing a tunnel in the snow, contain an allusion to Aladdin, a character in *The Thousand and One Nights*:

> With mittened hands, and caps drawn low,
> To guard our necks and ears from snow,
> We cut the solid whiteness through.
> And, where the drift was deepest, made
> Λ tunnel walled and overlaid
> With dazzling crystal: we had read
> Of rare Aladdin's wondrous cave,
> And to our own his name we gave.
> —John Greenleaf Whittier,
> from "Snow-Bound"

The cave in the tale contains a magic lamp that helps Aladdin discover vast riches. By alluding to Aladdin's cave, Whittier makes us see the icy tunnel in the snow as a magical, fairy-tale place.

See "Eruption: Pu'u O'o," page 140, lines 24–28.
The poet compares the land around the crater rim to a Leviathan.
See "The Legend," page 142, lines 45–46.
The poet alludes to an Asian legend about the night sky.

ANALOGY A comparison made between two things to show how they are alike. Writers often make analogies to show how something unfamiliar is like something well known or widely experienced. Analogies are often used by scientific writers to explain difficult concepts.

See "In Praise of Zigzags," page 14.
The poet uses an analogy to compare two sets of things: the way a girl does her homework and the way she does her chores; and the geometry of textbooks and the geometry of life.

See also *Metaphor, Simile*.

ATMOSPHERE The overall mood or emotion of a work of literature. A work's atmosphere can often be described with one or two adjectives, such as *scary, dreamy, happy, sad,* or *nostalgic.* A writer creates atmosphere by using images, sounds, and descriptions that convey a particular feeling.

See also *Mood.*

BALLAD A song or songlike poem that tells a story. Ballads usually tell stories of tragedy or adventure, using simple language and a great deal of repetition. They generally have regular rhythm and rhyme patterns that make them easy to memorize.

"The Cowboy's Lament," page 149, is a ballad.

CONNOTATION A meaning, association, or emotion suggested by a word, in addition to its dictionary definition, or denotation. Words that have similar denotations may have different connotations. For example, suppose you wanted to describe someone who rarely changes plans in the face of opposition. You could use either *determined* or *pigheaded* to describe the person. The two words have similar denotations, but *determined* has positive connotations and *pigheaded* has negative connotations. Connotations can be especially important in poetry.

See Poetry Notes in Study Guide, page 53.
See use of the word *still* in "The Eavesdropper," page 15, and the use of the word *cross* in "In Praise of Zigzags," page 14.

See also *Tone.*

DESCRIPTION The kind of writing that creates a clear image of something, usually by using details that appeal to one or more of the senses: sight, hearing, smell, taste, and touch. Description works through **images**, words that appeal to the five senses. Writers use description in all forms of writing—in fiction,

nonfiction, and poetry. Here is a description from a famous poem that has found a place in the hearts of readers everywhere. The writer's description appeals to the sense of sight, and sets the mood for his story.

> The wind was a torrent of darkness among
> the gusty trees,
> The moon was a ghostly galleon tossed
> upon cloudy seas,
> The road was a ribbon of moonlight over the
> purple moor,
> And the highwayman came riding—
> Riding—riding—
> The highwayman came riding, up to the old
> inn door.
> —Alfred Noyes,
> from "The Highwayman"

See "What Brings Us Out," page 45, lines 4–5, and lines 22–25.
See "St. Francis Speaks to Me at a Young Age," page 56, lines 1–5.

FIGURE OF SPEECH A word or phrase that describes one thing in terms of something else and is not literally true. Figures of speech always involve some sort of imaginative comparison between seemingly unlike things. The most common forms are **simile** ("My heart is like a singing bird"), **metaphor** ("The road was a ribbon of moonlight"), and **personification** ("The leaves were whispering in the night").

See also *Metaphor, Personification, Simile.*

FREE VERSE Poetry without a regular meter or a rhyme scheme. Poets writing in free verse try to capture the natural rhythms of ordinary speech. To create their music, poets writing in free verse may use internal rhyme, repetition, alliteration, and onomatopoeia. Free verse also frequently makes use of vivid imagery. The following poem in free verse effectively uses images and the repetition of words to describe the effects of a family's eviction for not paying rent:

The 1st

What I remember about that day
is boxes stacked across the walk
and couch springs curling through the air
and drawers and tables balanced on the curb
and us, hollering,
leaping up and around
happy to have a playground;

nothing about the emptied rooms
nothing about the emptied family
                                    —Lucille Clifton

See "Nikki-Rosa," page 98, "The Latest Latin Dance Craze," page 22, and "It Started," page 170.

See also *Poetry, Rhyme, Rhythm.*

IMAGERY Language that appeals to the senses—sight, hearing, touch, taste, and smell. Most images are visual—that is, they create pictures in the mind by appealing to the sense of sight. Images can also appeal to the senses of hearing, touch, taste, and smell. They can appeal to several senses at once. Though imagery is an element in all types of writing, it is especially important in poetry. The following poem is full of images about rain:

The Storm

In fury and terror
the tempest broke,
it tore up the pine
and shattered the oak,
yet the hummingbird hovered
within the hour
sipping clear rain
from a trumpet flower.
                                    —Elizabeth Coatsworth

See "Sleeping Father," page 58, line 1 and lines 9–10; "Tree," page 64, lines 12–13; and "The Air," page 65, lines 8–9.

IRONY A contrast between what is expected and what really happens. Irony can create powerful effects, from humor to horror. Here are some examples of situations that would make us feel a sense of irony:

- A shoemaker wears shoes with holes in them.
- The children of a famous dancer trip over their own feet.
- It rains on the day a group of weather forecasters have scheduled a picnic.
- Someone asks "How's my driving?" after going through a stop sign.
- A Great Dane runs away from a mouse.
- Someone living in the desert keeps a boat in her yard.
- A relative of a police officer robs a bank.
- Someone walks out in the midst of a hurricane and says, "Nice day."

See "Highway: Michigan," page 26, line 10, for the ironic use of the verb *toy*.
See the use of irony in the titles of "Who Burns for the Perfection of Paper," page 29 and "Courthouse Graffiti for Two Voices, " page 28.

LYRIC POEM A poem that expresses the feelings or thoughts of a speaker rather than telling a story. Lyric poems can express a wide range of emotions, from deep admiration to amusement. Lyric poems are usually short and imply, rather than directly state, a strong emotion.

See also *Narrative Poem.*

METAPHOR A comparison between two unlike things in which one thing becomes another thing. An **extended metaphor** carries the comparison through an entire work. A metaphor is an important type of figure of speech. Metaphors are used in all forms of writing and are common in ordinary speech. When you say about your grumpy friend "He's such a bear today," you do not mean that he is growing bushy black fur. You mean that he is in a bad mood and ready to attack, just the way a bear might be.

Metaphors differ from **similes**, which use specific words, such as *like, as, than*, and *resembles*, to make their comparisons. "He is behaving like a bear" is a simile.

Sometimes a writer hints at a connection instead of stating it directly. T. S. Eliot uses an **implied metaphor** in one of his poems when he describes fog as rubbing its back on windows, making a sudden leap, and curling around a house to fall asleep. By using words that we associate with a cat's behavior, Eliot implies a comparison without stating "The fog is a cat."

An **extended metaphor** is a metaphor that is extended, or developed, over several lines of writing or even throughout an entire work.

See "Eruption: Pu'u O'o," page 140–41, lines 23–27 and "Wolves," page 87, lines 5–7.

See also *Figure of Speech, Personification, Simile.*

MOOD The overall emotion created by a work of literature. A work of literature can often be described with one or more adjectives: *sad, scary, hopeful, exciting*, and so on. These are description of the work's mood—its emotional atmosphere.

See "Old Christmas," pages 156–58, which creates a mood that is haunting or eerie.

See also *Atmosphere.*

NARRATIVE POEM A poem that tells a story. "Flannan Isle," pages 134–37 and "Eruption: Pu'u O'o," pages 140–41 are narrative poems.

ONOMATOPOEIA The use of words with sounds that echo their sense. Onomatopoeia (än'ō•mat'ō•pē'ə) is so natural to us that we use it at a very early age. *Buzz, rustle, boom, tick tock, tweet*, and *bark* are all examples of onomatopoeia. Onomatopoeia is an important element in creating the music of poetry. In the following lines the poet creates a frenzied mood by choosing words that imitate the sounds of alarm bells:

> Oh, the bells, bells, bells!
> What a tale their terror tells
> Of Despair!
> How they clang, and clash, and roar!
> What a horror they outpour
> On the bosom of the palpitating air!
> Yet the ear, it fully knows
> By the twanging
> And the clanging
> How the danger ebbs and flows.
> —Edgar Allan Poe,
> from "The Bells"

See "Crossing," page 6, in which onomatopoeia and alliteration are used to mimic moving freight cars.

See also *Alliteration.*

ORAL TRADITION A collection of folk tales, songs, and poems that have been passed on orally from generation to generation.

PERSONIFICATION A figure of speech in which a nonhuman thing or quality is talked about as if it were human. In the following lines, the wind is spoken of as a man:

> The wind—tapped like a tired Man—
> And like a Host—"Come in"
> —Emily Dickinson,
> from "The Wind Tapped
> Like a Tired Man"

See "the sonnet-ballad," page 74, lines 6–12, in which the speaker personifies death.

See also *Figure of Speech, Metaphor, Simile*.

POETRY A kind of rhythmic, compressed language that uses figures of speech and imagery designed to appeal to emotion and imagination. We know poetry when we see it because it is usually arranged in a particular way on the page. Traditional poetry often has a regular pattern of rhythm **(meter)** and may have a regular **rhyme scheme**. **Free verse** is poetry that has no regular rhythm or rhyme. The major forms of poetry are the **lyric** (a songlike poem that expresses a speaker's feelings) and the **narrative** (a poem that tells a story). Two popular narrative forms are the **epic** and the **ballad**.

See also *Figure of Speech, Free Verse, Imagery, Refrain, Rhyme, Rhythm, Speaker, Stanza*.

POINT OF VIEW The vantage point from which a story is told. The most common points of view are the **omniscient,** the **third-person limited,** and the **first person.**

1. In the **omniscient,** or all-knowing, **point of view** the narrator or speaker knows everything about the characters and their problems.

2. In the **third-person limited point of view,** the narrator or speaker focuses on the thoughts and feelings of only one character.

3. In the **first-person point of view,** one of the characters, using the personal pronoun *I,* is telling the story.

REFRAIN A group of words repeated at intervals in a poem, song, or speech. Refrains are usually associated with songs and poems, but they are also used in speeches and other forms of literature. Refrains are most often used to create rhythm, but they may also provide emphasis or commentary, create suspense, or help hold a work together. Refrains may be repeated with small variations in a work in order to fit a particular context or to create a special effect.

See "Backwater Blues," page 160, the first two lines in each stanza.

RHYME The repetition of accented vowel sounds and all sounds following them in words close together in a poem. *Mean* and *screen* are rhymes, as are *crumble* and *tumble*. Rhyme has many purposes in poetry: It creates rhythm, lends a songlike quality, emphasizes ideas, organizes the poem (for instance, into stanzas or couplets), provides humor or delight for the reader, and makes the poem memorable.

Many poems—for example, "Valentine," page 10—use **end rhymes**, rhymes at the end of a line.

Internal rhymes are rhymes within lines. The following line has an internal rhyme (*turning/burning*):

> Back into the chamber turning, all my soul within me burning
> —Edgar Allan Poe,
> from "The Raven"

Rhyming sounds need not be spelled the same way; for instance, *gear/here* forms a rhyme. Rhymes can involve more than one syllable or more than one word; *poet/know it* is an example. Rhymes involving sounds that are similar but not exactly the same are called **slant rhymes** (or **near rhymes** or **approximate rhymes**). *Leave/live* is an example of a slant rhyme. Poets writing in English often use slant rhymes because English is not a very rhymable language. It has many words that rhyme with no other word (*orange*) or with only one other word (*mountain/fountain*). Poets interested in how a poem looks on the printed page sometimes use **eye rhymes**, or **visual rhymes**—rhymes involving words that are spelled similarly but are pronounced differently. *Tough/Cough* is an eye rhyme. (*Tough/rough* is a "real" rhyme.)

The pattern of end rhymes in a poem is called a **rhyme scheme**. To indicate the rhyme scheme of a poem, use a separate letter of the alphabet for each rhyme. For example, the rhyme scheme of "Valentine" is *abcb*.

See also *Free Verse, Poetry, Rhythm.*

RHYTHM A musical quality produced by the repetition of stressed and unstressed syllables or by the repetition of certain other sound patterns. Rhythm occurs in all language—written and spoken—but is particularly important in poetry.

The most obvious kind of rhythm is the regular pattern of stressed and unstressed syllables that is found in some poetry. This pattern is called **meter**. In the following lines describing a cavalry charge, the rhythm echoes the galloping of the attackers' horses:

> The Assyrian came down like the wolf on the fold,
> And his cohorts were gleaming in purple and gold;
> And the sheen of their spears was like stars on the sea,
> When the blue wave rolls nightly on deep Galilee.
>
> —George Gordon, Lord Byron,
> from "The Destruction of
> Sennacherib"

Marking the stressed (′) and unstressed (˘) syllables in a line is called **scanning** the line. Lord Byron's scanned lines show a rhythmic pattern in which two unstressed syllables are followed by a stressed syllable. Read the lines aloud and listen to this rhythmic pattern. Also, notice how the poem's end rhymes help create the rhythm.

Writers can also create rhythm by repeating words and phrases or even by repeating whole lines and sentences.

See also *Free Verse, Poetry, Rhyme.*

SIMILE A comparison between two unlike things using a word such as *like, as, than,* or *resembles.* The simile (sĭm′ə•lē) is an important figure of speech. "His voice is as loud as a trumpet" and "Her eyes are like the blue sky" are similes.

See "Mango," page 76, lines 7–8, and "My Grandfather's Hat," page 80, lines 17–20.

See also *Figure of Speech, Metaphor.*

SPEAKER The voice talking in a poem. Sometimes the speaker is identical to the poet, but often the speaker and the poet are not the same. The poet may be speaking as a child, a woman, a man, an animal, or even an object.

See also *Poetry.*

STANZA In a poem, a group of consecutive lines that forms a single unit. A stanza in a poem is something like a paragraph in prose; it often expresses a unit of thought. A stanza may consist of any number of lines. In some poems each stanza has the same rhyme scheme.

See also *Poetry, Rhyme.*

SYMBOL A person, a place, a thing, or an event that has its own meaning *and* stands for something beyond itself as well. Examples of symbols are all around us—in music, on television, and in everyday conversation. The skull and crossbones, for example, is a symbol of danger; the dove is a symbol of peace; and the red rose stands for true love. In literature, symbols are often more personal.

See "Mango," pages 76–77. The mango stored in the clay jar represents the speaker in the poem.

TONE The attitude that a writer takes toward the audience, a subject, or a character. Tone is conveyed through the writer's choice of words and details.

See "Hector the Collector," page 4, which is light and humorous in tone or "The Portrait," page 70, which is serious in tone.

Index of Authors and Titles

Acknowledgments

For permission to reprint copyrighted material, grateful acknowledgment is made to the following sources:

Indran Amirthanayagam: Autobiographical comments by Indran Amirthanayagam. Copyright © 2003 by Indran Amirthanayagam. "The Elephants Are in the Yard" by Indran Amirthanayagam.

Arte Público Press: "Fences" from *Communion* by Pat Mora. Copyright © 1991 by Pat Mora. Published by Arte Público Press, University of Houston, 1991.

Asian Studies Center, Michigan State University: "Poeti-c Art" by Arudra.

Catherine Beston Barnes: "The Storm" by Elizabeth Coatsworth.

Bilingual Press, Hispanic Research Center, Arizona State University, Tempe, AZ 85287-2702: "My Grandfather's Hat" by Judith Ortiz Cofer from *Bilingual Review,* vol. 17, no. 2, 1992. Copyright © 1992 by Judith Ortiz Cofer.

Robert Bly: "Seeing the Eclipse in Maine" from *Morning Poems* by Robert Bly. Copyright © 1997 by Robert Bly. "Things My Brother and I Could Do" from *The Sibling Society* by Robert Bly. Copyright © 1996 by Robert Bly.

BOA Editions, Ltd.: From "the 1st," "in the inner city" and "the bodies broken on" from *Good Woman: Poems and a Memoir 1969–1980* by Lucille Clifton. Copyright © 1987 by Lucille Clifton. "4 daughters" and "why some people be mad at me sometimes" from *Next: New Poems* by Lucille Clifton. Copyright © 1987 by Lucille Clifton. "I Ask My Mother to Sing" from *Rose* by Li-Young Lee. Copyright © 1986 by Li-Young Lee.

The Estate of Gwendolyn Brooks: "the sonnet-ballad" from *Blacks* by Gwendolyn Brooks. Copyright © 1991 by Gwendolyn Brooks.

Rosemary Catacalos: Autobiographical comments by Rosemary Catacalos. Copyright © 2003 by Rosemary Catacalos. "Morning Geography" by Rosemary Catacalos from *Colorado Review,* Fall 1993. Also published in *Paper Dance: 55 Latino Poets* (Persea, 1995) and *Floricanto Sí! A Collection of Latina Poetry* (Penguin, 1998).

Siv Cedering: "The Changeling" by Siv Cedering. Copyright © 1998 by Siv Cedering.

Vic Coccimiglio: Autobiographical comments by Vic Coccimiglio. Copyright © 2003 by Vic Coccimiglio. "St. Francis Speaks to Me at a Young Age" by Vic Coccimiglio. Copyright © 1996 by Vic Coccimiglio.

Coffee House Press: "Problems with Hurricanes" from *Red Beans* by Victor Hernández Cruz. Copyright © 1991 by Victor Hernández Cruz.

Copper Canyon Press, P.O. Box 271, Port Townsend, WA 98368-0271: "move" and "my lost father" from *The Book of Light* by Lucille Clifton. Copyright © 1993 by Lucille Clifton.

Crown Publishers, a division of Random House, Inc.: "Emergency Situation" from *Mother Said* by Hal Sirowitz. Copyright © 1996 by Hal Sirowitz.

Victor Hernández Cruz: "The Latest Latin Dance Craze" from *Tropicalization* by Victor Hernández Cruz. Copyright © 1976 by Victor Hernández Cruz.

Doubleday, a division of Random House, Inc.: "Highway: Michigan" from *The Collected Poems of Theodore Roethke.* Copyright 1940 by Theodore Roethke.

Firebrand Books, Milford Connecticut: From "All the Women Caught in Flaring Light" from *Crime Against Nature* by Minnie Bruce Pratt. Copyright © 1990 by Minnie Bruce Pratt.

Maria Mazziotti Gillan: "In New Jersey Once" from *Where I Come From: Selected and New Poems* by Maria Mazziotti Gillan. Copyright © 1995 by Maria Mazziotti Gillan.

Nikki Giovanni: "Nikki-Rosa" from *Black Judgement* by Nikki Giovanni. Copyright © 1968 by Nikki Giovanni.

David R. Godine, Publisher, Inc.: "Bells" and "Day's Blood" by Jimmy Santiago Baca from *After Aztlan,* edited by Ray González. Copyright © 1992 by Ray González.

Vince Gotera: "Beetle on a String" from *Flippin'* by Vince Gotera. Copyright © 1996 by Vince Gotera. Published by the Asian American Writers' Workshop.

Donald Hall: "Valentine" from *Exiles and Marriages* by Donald Hall. Copyright © 1950, 1951, 1953, 1954, 1955 by Donald Hall.

HarperCollins Publishers Inc.: "Old Christmas" from *Lonesome Water* by Roy A. Helton. Copyright 1930 by Harper & Row, Publishers, Inc.; copyright renewed © 1958 by Roy A. Helton. "Hector the Collector" from *Where the Sidewalk Ends: The Poems and Drawings of Shel Silverstein.* Copyright © 1974 by Evil Eye Music, Inc.

Harvard University Press and the Trustees of Amherst College: From "The Wind Tapped Like a Tired Man" from *The Poems of Emily Dickinson,* edited by Thomas H. Johnson. Copyright © 1951, 1955, 1979, 1983 by the President and Fellows of Harvard College. Published by The Belknap Press of Harvard University Press, Cambridge, Mass.

Henry Holt and Company, LLC: "I Was Sleeping Where the Black Oaks Move" from *Jacklight* by Louise Erdrich. Copyright © 1984 by Louise Erdrich.

Houghton Mifflin Company: "Ox Cart Man" from *Old and New Poems* by Donald Hall. Copyright © 1990 by Donald Hall. All rights reserved. "The Air," "Childhood of the Ancients," and "Tree" from *The Glass Hammer: A Southern Childhood* by Andrew Hudgins. Copyright © 1994 by Andrew Hudgins. All rights reserved.

Alfred A. Knopf, a division of Random House, Inc.: "Eruption: Pu'u O'o" and "The Legend" from *The River of Heaven* by Garrett Hongo. Copyright © 1988 by Garrett Hongo. "Juke Box Love Song" from *The Collected Poems* of Langston Hughes. Copyright © 1994 by The Estate of Langston Hughes.

Christian Langworthy: "Mango" by Christian Langworthy.

Hal Leonard Corporation: Lyrics to "Backwater Blues" by Bessie Smith. Copyright © 1927 and renewed © 1974 by Frank Music Corporation. All rights reserved.

Liveright Publishing Corporation: "All in green went my love riding" from *Complete Poems: 1904–1962* by E. E. Cummings, edited by George J. Firmage. Copyright 1923, 1951, 1956, 1984, 1991 by the Trustees for the E. E. Cummings Trust; copyright © 1976 by George J. Firmage.

Macmillan, London, UK: "Flannan Isle" by Wilfrid Wilson Gibson.

Mellen Poetry Press: "Sleeping Father" from *The China Cupboard and the Coal Furnace* by David Chin. Copyright © 1999 by Mellen Poetry Press.

Janice Mirikitani: "For My Father" from *Awake in the River* by Janice Mirikitani. Copyright © 1978 by Janice Mirikitani. Published by Isthmus Press.

New Directions Publishing Corp.: "It Started" from *Immigrants in Our Own Land* by Jimmy Santiago Baca. Copyright © 1982 by Jimmy Santiago Baca. "Meditations on the South Valley, Part VI" from *Martin and Meditations on the South Valley* by Jimmy Santiago Baca. Copyright © 1987 by Jimmy Santiago Baca.

W. W. Norton & Company, Inc.: "Courthouse Graffiti for Two Voices" and "Who Burns for the Perfection of Paper" from *City of Coughing and Dead Radiators* by Martin Espada. Copyright © 1993 by Martin Espada. "The Portrait" from *Passing Through: The Later Poems* by Stanley Kunitz. Copyright © 1971, 1995 by Stanley Kunitz.

Naomi Shihab Nye: "My Father and the Fig Tree" and "Linked" by Naomi Shihab Nye. "What Brings Us Out" by Naomi Shihab Nye. Copyright © 1989 by Naomi Shihab Nye. First appeared in *The Georgia Review.* "So Far" (appeared as "Lost" in *Fuel*) by Naomi Shihab Nye. Copyright © 1998 by Naomi Shihab Nye. "The Lost Parrot" and "Hugging the Jukebox" from *Hugging the Jukebox* by Naomi Shihab Nye. Copyright © 1982 by Naomi Shihab Nye.

Marian Reiner: Six haiku from *Cricket Songs: Japanese Haiku,* translated by Harry Behn. Copyright © 1964 by Harry Behn and Peter Behn; copyright renewed © 1992 by Prescott Behn, Pamela Behn Adam, and Peter Behn.

University of Pittsburgh Press: "Flying at Night" from *One World at a Time* by Ted Kooser. Copyright © 1985 by Ted Kooser. "At the End of the Weekend," "First Snow," "Selecting a Reader," and "Year's End" from *Sure Signs: New and Selected Poems* by Ted Kooser. Copyright © 1980 by Ted Kooser.

University of Texas Press: "The Ballad of Gregorio Cortez" from *With His Pistol in His Hand: A Border Ballad and Its Hero* by Américo Paredes. Copyright © 1958 and renewed © 1986 by Américo Paredes.

Viking Penguin, a division of Penguin Putnam Inc.: "Crossing" from *Letter from a Distant Land* by Philip Booth. Copyright 1953 by Philip Booth.

Jane O. Wayne: "The Eavesdropper" from *Looking Both Ways: Poems* by Jane Wayne. Copyright © 1984 by Jane Wayne. Published by the University of Missouri Press. "In Praise of Zigzags: For a Girl Failing Geometry" by Jane O. Wayne. Copyright © 1985 by Jane O. Wayne.

Wesleyan University Press: "Wolves" from *The Stone Harp* by John Haines. Copyright © 1968 by John Haines. "If the Owl Calls Again" from *Winter News* by John Haines. Copyright © 1966 by John Haines. "Facing It" from *Dien Cau Dau* by Yusef Komunyakaa. Copyright © 1989 by Yusef Komunyakaa. "Banking Potatoes" from *Magic City* by Yusef Komunyakaa. Copyright © 1992 by Yusef Komunyakaa.

West End Press, Albuquerque, New Mexico: "Taking a Visitor to See the Ruins" and "What the Moon Said" from *Skin and Bones: Poems 1979–87* by Paula Gunn Allen. Copyright © 1988 by Paula Gunn Allen.

Cited Source:

From "Fragments" by Philip Booth from *Ploughshares*, Spring 1991. Published by Emerson College, Boston, 1991.

Photo Credits

Page 5, AP/Wide World Photos; 8, Courtesy of Philip Booth/Photo by Tom Stewart; 12, Courtesy of Donald Hall; 16, Courtesy of Jane O. Wayne/Photo by Hans Levi; 20, Getty News Images; 25, Courtesy of Coffee House Press/Photo by Chris Felven; 27, Getty News Images; 30, Kevin Gutting/AP/Wide World Photos; 33, Courtesy of Hal Sirowitz/Photo by Matt Valentine; 36, Courtesy of Vince Gotera; 38, Courtesy of Naomi Shihab Nye/Photo James H. Evans; 39, Courtesy of Naomi Shihab Nye; 54, Courtesy of Siv Cedering; 57, Courtesy of Vic Coccimiglio; 59, Courtesy of David Chin; 62, Courtesy of Janice Mirikitani; 67, Courtesy of Andrew Hudgins; 69, Courtesy of Li-Young Lee/Photo by Donna Lee; 71, Getty News Images; 73, CORBIS; 75, AP/Wide World Photos; 78, Courtesy of Christian Langworthy; 81, Courtesy of Arte Publico Press; 85, James Keyser/Timepix; 88, Courtesy of Wesleyan University Press; 90, Courtesy of Ted Kooser; 91, Courtesy of Ted Kooser; 100, Getty News Images; 103, Courtesy of Arte Publico Press; 106, Thomas Victor/Timepix; 109, Courtesy of Maria Mazziotti Gillan; 112, Coutesy of Indran Amirthanayagam; 116, Courtesy of Rosemary Catacalos/Photo by Carlos Rene Perez; 122, Natasha Lane/AP/Wide World Photos; 124, Mark Lennihan/AP/Wide World Photos; 138, HRW Photo Research Library; 144, Courtesy of Wesleyan University Press; 154, Bettmann/CORBIS; 161, Hulton Archive/Getty Images; 168, Frank Eyers/AP/Wide World Photos.